C000254928

DE$~~~~

BIKING

A Guide to Independent Motorcycling in the Sahara

by Chris Scott

Illustrations by Alan Bradshaw
and maps by Peter Corbett

With contributions by Peter Corbett, Alisdair Kennedy
and Si Melber

Published by the Travellers' Bookshop, 25 Cecil Court, London WC2N 4EZ

Author's acknowledgments

Thanks to Jules Brown for editing the original text, Alan Bradshaw for sketches and proof reading and Peter Corbett for maps and more proof reading. At Rough Guides thanks to Martin Dunford and Richard Trillo for use of town maps. Thanks also to Robert Strauss of Compass Star Publications for advice and to *Motorcycle International* and *SuperBike* magazines for permission to reproduce articles.

Finally I should like to thank Lucinda Boyle and Sally Newman at the Travellers' Bookshop and the resources of Bernard Shapero Books for supporting this publication.

All photographs by Chris Scott unless otherwise credited.
Back cover: top two photos A. Humphrey

Cover design by Sonja Howick.
Design and page layout by Alan Spicer.

Printed by Antony Rowe Ltd., Chippenham, Wilts. UK.
Copyright © Chris Scott 1995.

All the advice and recommendations given in this book have been gathered from personal experience, but the dangers of riding around the Sahara on a motorbike have also been clearly stressed. Recognise your limitations and risks you are taking. No responsibility can be taken by the author, contributors or the publisher for misfortunes or loss that may occur while motorcycling in remote or dangerous regions. The original edition of this book was prepared before the current development of civil unrest in Algeria. Read the warning on page 100 and check on the latest situation before considering a visit to this country.

First published December 1993.
This second edition published September 1995.
A CIP catalogue record of this book is available from the British Library.
ISBN 1 87447 2017

CONTENTS

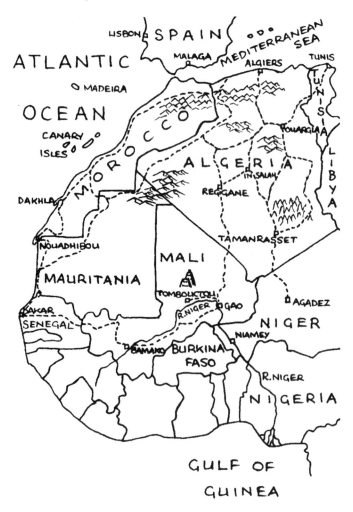

The Sahara and West Africa

INTRODUCTION

Holden: *You're in a desert, walking along in the sand when all of a sudden you look down –*
Leon: *– What one?*
Holden: *What!?*
Leon: *What desert?*
Holden: *Doesn't make any difference what desert, it's completely hypothetical.*
Leon: *Then how come I'd be there?*
Holden: *Maybe you're fed up, maybe you wanna be by yourself, who knows?*

BLADE RUNNER

TONIGHT ABOUT 10pm, a Motorail train leaves Paris bound for Marseille. By 8am tomorrow morning, following a good night's rest and a free snack, you'll be on your way to the port at La Joliette from where a ferry leaves for Algiers at midday. Around late-afternoon the following day you will have somehow muddled your way through the Algerian customs and following a few false starts in the city, you will be on the N1 riding south over the Atlas Mountains to Ghardaia, a day or two away.

And Ghardaia friends, is the gateway to the Sahara and the last big town you will be seeing for a couple of weeks. Turn left for the Tassili plateau and Djanet, carry straight on for Tamanrasset and the Hoggar. Everything thins out from here: traffic, vegetation, settlements. Tongues of sand begin to appear across the road and are a real danger on a bike if taken too fast. Camels wandering close to the roadside should also be treated with caution. If you are heading directly for Tamanrasset, you could be riding on newly-repaired tarmac all the way, but don't count on it. By the time you get to 'Tam' (as it's known) you will have already learned a lot about travelling in the desert.

My first trip to the Sahara in 1982 was well planned, but turned out to be a shambles. Information on what to expect, and especially bike preparation, was hard to come by. In those days, it was the adventurous optimist who bodged up his XT/XL or BMW and set off across the desert with an alloy tank, a rack welded on by a friend, spare tyres and far too much baggage.

Back then I had the feeling of riding into an abyss and secretly knew my overloaded pile of junk (an XT500, naturally) would barely make it across the desert to West Africa. In fact, it never did.

But why go?

Perhaps I'm worse off for living in the south of England but you must admit that non-competitive off-road riding in this country is hardly challenging. I've spent many a memorable weekend squeezing Welsh bogs out of air filters, but it's just not the same as spending three days riding the distance from Penzance to Newcastle and seeing no signs of civilisation other than a couple of vehicles a day. Everything you need to complete that journey safely is carried with you and it will all be done without eliciting the scorn of ramblers, farmers or the Police. You won't even have to *cross* that bit of tarmac to make that RUPP meet that BOAT*.

Come the evening, pick a friendly looking dune and set up camp under the brightest night sky you've ever seen. Once you've fed yourself and done your other chores, snuggle into your sleeping bag and count the shooting stars, hoping that the gerbils keep out of your Alpen. Next morning you might see a caravan of nomads pass silently by on the other side of the valley, the women wrapped in veils sitting motionlessly on the backs of the camels. The Ridgeway this isn't!

As big as Australia and only a few days away, for the adventurous biker the reasons for choosing the Sahara are clear. This guidebook chiefly concerns itself with preparing you and your bike to visit the central Saharan countries of Mauritania, Algeria, Niger and Mali. In all these countries French is spoken as well as the indigenous tongues; some share the same currency; and West Africa itself lacks only the vast reserves of game that make East Africa so appealing. While the practical advice offered here is valid for adventurous off-road biking anywhere, I have limited the itineraries to the areas with which I have become familiar over the last fifteen years.

Crossing the Sahara, like crossing the Atlantic, has been successfully accomplished by many people. The shortest crossing between tarmac can involve less than 300 miles of off-road riding. But, as with crossing the ocean, any trip could be your last: The Sahara does not suffer fools. Even with the best preparation and most cautious attitude you will be lucky to get away without a bark, if not a full-blown bite. And any over-ambitious plans will soon be brought put into perspective when you first venture off the road with a fully loaded bike.

---

* RUPP: 'Road Used as Public Path'. BOAT: 'Byway Open to All Traffic' These are abbreviations for unsealed vehicular rights of way in England.

Photo: A. Humphrey

Make no mistake, when things start going wrong out there it can be a nightmare.

Alone on a motorcycle you are more vulnerable and, at the same time, more accessible to the events that can make or break your trip. On a bike, the lack of metal and glass which protects and isolates car occupants, can add an edge to desert biking that may not be to everyone's taste. In my experience, however, the locals in the Sahara have a certain admiration for bikers and the hardships they clearly endure, perhaps seeing bike riders as closer to their own nomadic origins. Expect your itinerary - conceived on the living room floor with a couple of cans and all the chairs pushed back - to go to pieces once you're there. But also be aware that the more complex the problems you face, the more ingenious your solutions, and the more innovative your skills. They have to be. It goes without saying that you are truly on your own in the desert. Insurance is only academic when you're two hundred kilometres from help with a broken shoulder.

This is what counts: A manageable, economical, reliable and comfortable bike that can carry you and your gear over rack-breaking corrugations, rim-denting rocks and power-sapping sand, non-stop, for half a week at a time. Throughout, you must have the mental stamina to deal with all the usual stressful situations of getting lost, making emergency repairs or falling out with your companions.

Most first-timers tend to overestimate their personal needs and underestimate the hammering their bike will receive while carrying all those needs. There are no short cuts when preparing your vehicle for a desert trip, which is why most people carry on over to West, East or South Africa - by the time you've made it across the Sahara you may as well carry on. But for most people, especially those on motorbikes, the Sahara will be the most memorable part of the trip. The awe inspiring solitude and freedom experienced on a bike, emphasised by the vast landscapes and distant horizons, create a feeling of well-being which is unique to the desert. It is rare to meet anyone who has visited the Sahara who has not, at some time, talked about going back.

A BIKE FOR THE TRIP

AN IDEAL DESERT BIKE should be light, economical and have an engine that offers a broad and predictable spread of power. It should have a proven frame, suspension, transmission and wheels, as all these components will be getting a hammering as well as having to cope with the added stress of extra weight. The machine should also be comfortable and be capable of carrying at least 30 litres of fuel plus up to 50 kilos of water, food, spares and personal baggage. With all this weight it should retain at least some agility in sandy or rocky terrain, where good ground clearance will be a further asset.

The type of bike that fulfils most of these criteria most of the time is a large capacity, single cylinder, four-stroke trail bike. Indeed 600cc singles far outnumber any other type of bike used in the Sahara without support.

Road Bikes, Trail Bikes and Rally Replicas

It should appear obvious that road bikes only serve to make a tiring and potentially hazardous trip even more so. Road bikes are exhausting to ride off-road at the best of times and, in one case I witnessed, the ungainly BMW suffered a series of small crashes that ended up destroying the machine altogether.

Trail bikes on the other hand, have genuinely useful features, such as folding foot controls, 21" front wheels with steering geometry to match, and greater ground clearance. And, to a certain extent, they are designed to be dropped without suffering major damage.

In the early 1980's the growing popularity of the Paris–Dakar Rally caught the imagination of the world's bike manufacturers. It gave rise to a genre of 'rally replica' bikes whose large tanks, simple yet tractable engines, and plush suspension were ideal for adventurous off-road touring. Below, there's a general round-up of the makes and models available which should assist you in your choice

Yamaha

Probably the most popular range of bikes used in the desert is Yamaha's
XT series, specifically the 600cc (now 660cc) Ténéré version. The original kick-start Ténérés were everything that earlier, much modified,
XT500's tried to be. Standard equipment included a 27 litre fuel tank, 'o'
ring chain, powerful brakes and lights, an oil cooler and
motocross–derived suspension, all wrapped around a simple air-cooled,
four-stroke single cylinder engine based on the exceptionally economical XT550. With only minimal alterations, early model Ténérés still
make excellent and reliable machines for desert travel. (There's an
unusual anomaly that the air-cooled electric start Ténérés tend to experience in Africa, possibly as a result of the poor fuel. The exhaust baffles
in the silencer tend to block up with sludge after several thousand miles
creating a loss of power that feels much like fuel starvation. Jonny Bealby
experienced this in Ethiopia (see *Running with the Moon* in 'Books') and
so did I and another Ténéré rider I met later in Algeria. After the usual
fuel line checks we each feared the worse – a knackered engine but
without the usual sound effects. The solution, which came to us all
sooner or later, was simply to bang some alternative exhaust holes in
the silencer end or cut it off, giving an instant return of free-flowing
power.)

Subsequent models have gradually moved away from this ideal
despite some detail improvements (notably in the positioning of the oil
tank and cooler, and greater air filter capacity). Electric starts, rear disc
brakes and fairings have all been paid for by retrograde cost-cutting features elsewhere. Although the original kick-start Ténéré's undersprung
suspension was greatly improved, these late models appear to be less
mechanically durable and less economical

The latest 660cc version of the Ténéré is an attempt to integrate the
design modifications of the past few models around a new, five-valve
water-cooled engine. Yamaha's usual high attention to detail is apparent.
The vulnerable water pump is protected by an extension of the bash-
plate and it would take quite a knock to damage the radiator beyond
repair. The XT660 is some 30kg heavier than the first XT600Z but,
apart from the cost, it is a superior machine to the models which immediately preceded it.

The XT350 is an ideal compromise between light weight and adequate power, but even on the road it lacks the solid feel of the larger
XTs and certainly misses the low-down punch that makes the bigger
bikes so easy to ride in power-sapping conditions. Nevertheless, this

Honda XL600LM. (M.Spencer)

model may suit smaller riders or women; i.e., those who feel uncomfortable with the seat height of the larger capacity machines. The soft suspension would require preloading to cope with the extra weight, but even then the 350 is only 15-20% more economical than a 600.

Honda

Honda has a broadly similar and popular XL series of trail bikes, particularly the short-lived XL600LM with its large tank. Things started coming together with the introduction of the XL500R (Pro-Link) model. Early XLMs had unreliable electric starters and sometimes started poorly with the kick-starter, but all XLs tend to run better than Ténérés on low octane fuel.

No large capacity single is going to be as smooth as a multi-cylinder engine but XLMs are comparatively lumpy at low revs, which can tire the rider and accelerate the wear of the transmission. The paradoxical trend for tubeless tyres on (albeit nominally) dual-purpose machines started with XLMs. Tubeless tyres cannot be reliably repaired on the piste and for this reason inner tubes should be fitted. The street-scrambling NX650 Dominator is popularly considered as one of the best all-round big singles with a great engine and handling to match. It's almost too good to load down with junk and take to the desert where all its racy qualities would be smothered. The smallish tank would need enlarging or replacing (23 litre Acerbis unit available).

Suzuki

Less common in the Sahara are Suzuki DR four-stroke singles. Since the original DR400, capacities have gone up and down: from 600cc rally clones to the odd and overweight DR800S and, at present, the excellent little DR350S and less purposeful but still suitable DR650RSE. Engines and components are basically similar to their contemporaries, that is; four-valve overhead cams; progressive rate single-shock rear suspension; and 12 volt electrics. Owners of XT500s especially will appreciate this last innovation! DR600s tend to be a little sportier than Hondas or Yamahas, with sharper handling and more responsive power. However, their greater fuel consumption and relatively poorer reliability, as well as Suzuki's inferior build quality may be why they have never caught on in the Sahara.

Nevertheless Suzukis are notably cheaper than their competitors, and you can buy a new DR650RSE for around 20% less than an XT660. The DR650RSE has a nearly-useful 20 litre fuel tank, a fairing and Suzuki's own 'SACS' cooling system - basically a large capacity oil cooler and pump, far preferable to the complexities of an XT660's water-cooling system.

The DR350 makes a more functional desert bike than an XT350 but has the same limitations already mentioned, i.e. with less torque at low revs, and built for lightness and agility as an off-road playbike. Despite their temptingly large tanks, DR750s and 800s are nearly as heavy as some twin cylinder machines but undoubtedly not as smooth. If you plan on taking a Suzuki, stick with the more popular 600–650 models.

Kawasaki

Virtually unknown in the Sahara are early Kawasaki 600 singles- fast, light, revvy and hopelessly unreliable. Avoid the kick-start ('A') model no matter how cheap it is. Later, electric start models struggled to overcome their predecessors' reputation and the short-lived KLR650 had, if nothing else, a 23 litre tank. Any prospective desert bike originally fitted with a useful (over 25 litre) tank is a large problem and expense already solved. The KLR650 was a sound machine with light steering and a spacious feel but soon it became the Tengai, the same bike enclosed in flashy bodywork offering no particular advantage on the piste and a horrible mess of broken bodywork when it crashes. The current KLR/KLX650 models are snazzy street bikes: light, fast and small tanked, they appear to lack the robustness a desert bike needs.

The vulnerability of a water-cooling system should always be borne in mind. Air–cooled singles, if in good condition, can cope perfectly well with desert conditions. An oil cooler can be fitted, if necessary. Mechanical simplicity is a distinct advantage in the desert.

European Singles

The only European singles worth considering are the 560cc Rotax-engined Tuareg Wind (no longer in production) from the Italian manufacturer Aprilia and BMW's bestselling F650 Funduro. The Tuareg Wind is similar in appearance to a Kawasaki Tengai, and very rare in this country. It's assembled from unusually high quality components and has many of the qualities you should seek in a competent desert bike. The non-metallic fuel tank may have been behind the reason for the limited importation of these high specification machines although plastic tanks are now legal in the UK as they are in most of Europe.

The odd-looking Funduro also uses a Rotax engine but is heavy for a 650cc bike. At 17.5 litres the tank is neither here nor there, although Acerbis do a 27 litre replacement. BMW's build quality has something going for it and the water-cooling gear is all neatly tucked in.

Another bike using a 500cc version of the Rotax engine is the Armstrong, as supplied to the British armed forces. Now in a less useful 350cc version, the old half-litre trail bikes can be picked up for under £1000 from certain outlets. The army may be hard on their vehicles but they also look after them and the Armstrong is built to take a hammering which unfortunately means it's fairly heavy for what it is. They also come with light pannier racks which could save a certain amount of work. With Rotax's solid reputation, a good version would make a tough, unsophisticated desert bike without spending heaps of money.

BMW Twins

From the beginning the most popular alternatives to the ubiquitous Japanese singles have been BMW's shaft-driven flat twins of 800,1000 and now 1100cc. So great is the world touring reputation of BMWs that it's not uncommon to see a desperately cumbersome road-oriented model struggling across the sands with a passenger on the back.

The dual-purpose 800 and 1000cc GS models do however, make the bulk easier to handle, as they have lighter steering, 21" front wheels, wider handlebars, altered gearing and weight saved wherever possible. The Boxer engines (as the flat twins are known) have unrivalled accessibility, simplicity and strength. However, they are heavier and use more fuel than single cylinder engines, partially due to the power–consuming effects of the shaft-drive final transmission

The weight and feel of a flat-twin BM gives a completely different ride to most other suitable bikes. Less agile but more comfortable, and with an unburstable engine, once loaded up and on the move the whole machine is reassuringly stable in a way big singles never are. Although BMWs are much heavier than singles of nearly similar capacity, their design puts most of the weight low down, creating a low centre of gravity and better stability.

The first R80GS came out nearly fifteen years ago and is now available at a secondhand price only slightly greater than a big single of similar age. From an off-road perspective, this model's shortcomings lie in its soft suspension, requiring either expensive replacement of forks, rear shock and swingarm or a gentler riding style - trail riding on a BMW demands this anyway. Inevitably a token 'Paris Dakar' version of the early GS was briefly produced with a much larger 32-litre fuel tank and a wider single seat with a rack immediately behind, but these models are very rare and the suspension remained unimproved.

In 1988, the R100GS was launched with a Paralever rear suspension linkage to counteract the shaft drive's inherent torque reaction under acceleration and deceleration. This has never really been a serious problem on shaft drive bikes; it's something you just get used to. However, the suspension and many other features were greatly improved and the whole bike was made physically much bigger than the old 800, whose low seat height is most reassuring when you begin to lose control of the machine.

The R100GS has a larger tank (but consumes still more fuel) and an oil cooler vulnerably mounted on the cylinder protection bars. It also has a small windscreen and much better suspension front and rear. If you can afford to buy and prepare such a machine (let alone handle it loaded up off-road) it's a luxurious way to travel in the desert, despite the weight penalty. Passengers will also have a more comfortable time on the back of a GS BMW than on most other machines. Current R100GS's have a fairing (with a Paris-Dakar variant still available) but have become faintly dual-purpose Euro-tourers rather than potentially purposeful desert bikes.

In 1993 the GS1100RG was introduced, a radical design exercise featuring telelever front suspension, fuel injection and about 25kg more weight over a R100GS. Undoubtedly someone will take such a bike on an extended off–road tour but the virtue of the earlier GS's was their simplicity, something which the R1100 seems to be deliberately moving away from in an attempt to keep up with Japanese innovation, of which more below.

Other Big Twins

In the last few years the 'rally replica' trend has moved in parallel with the genuine rally machines by fitting heavier, more powerful and complex twin cylinder engines from road bike models into trail bike frames. Honda's Transalp was the first of these 'Adventure Sports' bikes, with a smooth V-twin engine of 583cc derived from the VT road bike. Still available and much underrated, it has spawned the heavier, thirstier and more sophisticated 650 and 750 Africa Twin versions.

Yamaha have tried to get more mileage out of the best-selling Ténéré name by calling the their five-valve XTZ750cc twin a Super Ténéré. This popular bike, like the less common but reputedly better 650, 750 and current 900cc Elefant V–twins from Cagiva, it's a heavy and complex machine that falls some way away short of the original and perfectly adequate air-cooled singles. Its only virtue is that it offers the rider a whole lot more power as well as greater comfort in most conditions. This last factor is not an inconsequential asset on any bike as comfort is an important consideration if you intend riding daily for many weeks. Drawbacks, chiefly in fuel consumption from the highly tuned-engines and their greater weight, limit these types of bike to the main pistes.

ENDURO RACERS

Four-stroke enduro racing bikes, such as Honda XRs and Yamaha TTs, are not simply lighter and more powerful versions of their dual-purpose cousins. While it's true that, unloaded, these bikes are much more fun to ride off-road than trail bikes, they differ in other respects too. The lack of body work and other road-oriented ancilliaries may make them a good basis for a desert tourer, but the engines consume more fuel and require more attention due to their higher state of tune. Their spartan nature also extends to the narrow seat, intended to enable easy shifting of body weight during off-road events rather than for day-long support. In some cases, as with the KTM 600, with its excellent suspension and powerful engine, the close gearbox ratios designed for rapid response and acceleration can't be overcome by simply fitting a smaller sprocket at the rear wheel. You would still end up with a close bunch of ratios but with higher overall gearing. To be fair, a KTM is a more radical racer than an XR or TT and thus less likely to be seen in the desert unsupported. Again you must remember that by the time any bike is loaded up for a long off-road trip, all traces of nimbleness will have largely been eradicated.

SURVEY OF SUITABLE BIKES

THE FOLLOWING LIST is inevitably a personal selection of machines considered suitable for desert biking bearing in mind the factors discussed above, my experience in having ridden or owned most of them, and not least the cost of buying and preparing such a machine.

No attempt has been made to provide fuel consumption figures as baggage width, wind direction, the terrain and your riding style will all drastically affect normal fuel consumption. However, all of the bikes below ought to be able to achieve at least 50 mpg (on the road) if ridden with economy as a primary concern, many may achieve much more.

The weight is the dry weight, where known; otherwise it has been estimated as accurately as possible. With some of these bikes, just filling up the tank increases the weight by 20%. Wheel sizes have been provided as a guide to tyre fitment, and the petrol tank capacity indicated may in many cases, be the deciding factor between choosing one model or another.

- **APRILIA Tuareg Wind** (562cc); manufactured 1988–92; dry weight 148 kg; wheel sizes front 21", rear 17"; tank capacity 20 litres (approx). Has big tank and high specification equipment but is rarely found in this country. Body work inhibits radical modifications. Rotax engine is a bonus. Heavy for a single.

- **BMW F650 Funduro**; 1993; 189kg; 21"/17"; 17.5 l. BMW's new Rotax-engined, Italian-built street trail bike carries a lot more weight than similarly profiled machines but has a build quality that, with a bigger tank and the other usual mods, would make a good bike for the main pistes.

- **BMW R80GS**; 1980–88; 168kg; 21"/18"; 19 l (Paris-Dakar version 32 l). Early models are now numerous and cheap enough to modify economically. Simple mechanics, reliable reputation and comfortable, but the suspension needs uprating. Heavier and less fuel-efficient than just about all big singles.

- **BMW R80GS Paralever (R100GS)**; 1988; 215kg (220kg); 21 "/ 18" (tubeless tyres on both models); 24 l (26 l). Has many improvements over the old model, notably in suspension and brakes, but these models also have greater seat heights, are heavier and less fuel efficient, particularly the 1000cc model. These would be the bikes to use for two people to travel in reasonable comfort. Paris-Dakar versions are heavier still with crash bars, fairings, better brakes and bigger tanks (30 l +).

A much altered BMW based on a 60/6 motor and with huge
pannier tanks. BMWs adapt well to these sorts of modifications.

- **HONDA XL500R**; 1982–84; 132kg; 21"/17"; 10 l. Much improved version of
  the preceding 'S' model, with better suspension, steering and 12 volt
  electrics. Very economical but obviously needs a bigger tank.

- **HONDA XL600R**; 1985–86; 132kg; 21"/17"; 10 l. More powerful version of
  previous model with all its assets and the same tiny tank.

- **HONDA XL600LM**; 1985-89; 135kg; 21"/17" (tubeless tyres); 27 l. Honda's
  briefly-produced alternative to Yamaha's best-selling Ténéré but not so
  smooth and with an unreliable electric starter on early models (though
  these models also have a kick-starter). Seating position is more comfortable than on all Ténérés. If only all these (otherwise suitable) bikes had
  tanks as big as this.

- **KAWASAKI KLR650**; 1987-90; 147kg; 21'/17"; 23 l. Unpopular and
  short-lived model that has everything going for it, except water-cooling
  and the poor reputation of its 600cc predecessor. Feels light compared to
  a Ténéré and worth considering if one turns up at the right price.

- **SUZUKI DR350S**; 1990; 118kg; 21"/17"; 9 l. An enduro/playbike that is altogether too good to load down with luggage and take to the desert. Lacks
  the power of a 600cc and will not be as comfortable over a long day. 43 l
  Acerbis tank (for GS BMW's) has been made to fit. Best idea is to carry
  the gear in a car and enjoy the ride.

A cheap and cheerful Bénélé; a mixture of Honda CD and XLS, Yamaha RD and
Volkswagen Beetle.

- **SUZUKI DR600 Dakar or Raider**; 1984-90; 135kg; 21"/17"; 18/21 L.
  Mechanically similar to all other 600 singles but more powerful and with sharper handling than most. The tank is no great bonus as DR 600s tend to use
  more fuel than XLs or XTs. Also reliability (specifically the electrics) can be a
  problem.

- **SUZUKI DR650RSE**; 1991; 155kg; 21"/17"; 20 l. This new DR follows the trend
  for heavier, faired bikes with snazzy graphics. Basically a sound bike and much
  cheaper than the competition, but you get the finish and attention to detail you
  pay for. SACS cooling (see above under 'Suzuki') has something going for it.
  Good suspension.

- **YAMAHA XT350**; 1983; 120 kg; 21"/ 18"; 12 l. This bike may seem a good compromise between weight and power but XT350s are not really robust enough
  for a desert trip unless very lightly loaded. Same limitations as DR350, but inferior in most respects except fuel consumption and the cheap second-hand
  price.

- **YAMAHA XT500**; 1976-81; 140kg; 21"/18"; 11 l. The retro brigade would complain if I missed this one out, but the truth is that old XTs are dogs with feeble
  electrics and dated suspension. And they're not even cheap anymore! The best
  thing about XT 500s is the motor and low seat height, but all XTs have
  improved since then, including fuel consumption.

- **YAMAHA XT550**; 1982-84; 134kg; 21"/18"; 11.5l. Better than XT500s in all ways
  bar a flat spot in the carburetion. Very economical - this bike started the
  twin-carb trend which seems to work better on later singles. Smooth, but fairly
  rare second-hand. Rear suspension needs uprating for the desert.

- **YAMAHA XT600Z Ténéré**; 1982–87; 138kg; 21"/ 18"; 26.5 l. Once, if not still, the most popular bike in Sahara, the original white (in the UK) Ténéré is in some ways the best of the lot, especially as they are now fairly cheap second-hand. With firmer suspension and seat foam these bikes are ready to go. The later versions of this model, distinguished by slanting 'speed blocks' on the tank, are slightly better all round.

- **YAMAHA XT600ZE Ténéré**; 1987-90; 147kg; (152kg, faired models after '87); 21"/18"; 23 l. These models have slightly smaller tanks, firmer suspension and seats, and are heavier than the original Ténérés. Later ones have twin head lamp fairings. Rims, durability and fuel consumption are inferior, but the electric start is handy when stuck in soft sand.

- **YAMAHA XT660Z Ténéré**; 1991; 169kg; 21"/17"; 20 l. A much improved version of recent Ténérés, but 30kg heavier than the original and with a fairing and water-cooling. For the price of a new XT660 you could have a second-hand machine ready to go.

BIKE PREPARATION & MAINTENANCE

THOROUGH PREPARATION OF YOUR BIKE before you leave is just about the best assurance you can give yourself to a mechanically trouble–free trip. The longer time you spend riding your completed bike around at home the better. Ideally you want to start planning everything, including bike preparation, up to a year before departure so that you can ride out on the Big Day with complete confidence in your superbly prepared bike, if not in the road ahead. Try and do as much as you can by yourself or under close guidance so that you are familiar with your bike's workings. Things like engine rebuilds and welding can be left to trusted mechanics but changing wheels and tyres and cleaning air filters is something you want to be familiar with before you go.

As a general rule, if you doubt whether any component will last the entire length of your planned trip, renew it and finish off the partially used component once you've come back. This applies especially to things like tyres, chains and sprockets, which wear faster on a fully laden bike used off-road. Alternatively, on a longer, trans–continental trip, these sort of spares should be taken along or sent ahead.

If you are buying a new machine, it's best to buy it well in advance so that you are thoroughly familiar with its strengths and weaknesses before setting out. Lastly, bare in mind that modifications other than those recommended here may be necessary or useful on the machine of your choice.

Engine

It goes without saying that your engine should be in excellent condition before departure. It should be run in, recently serviced, oil-, air-, fuel- and water-tight, with ignition tuning spot on and cylinder compression to within 15% of the manufacturer's recommended figure. Excessive oil consumption in older engines should be rectified before departure. If you have rebuilt your engine, treating it with a teflon additive like 'Slick 50' can reap benefits, especially when starting from cold when most engine wear occurs.

Fuel Quality

Most modern, single cylinder engines have a relatively high compression ratio and, particularly Yamaha XT500s, run terribly on the low octane fuel you'll often find in Africa. Air-cooled engines in particular should always be served the highest octane fuel available - '*super*' as opposed to '*normale*' in Saharan West Africa. Unless you are off on a very long trip, it's not worth lowering the compression ratio (by fitting an extra base gasket, for example), with the consequent alteration in ignition timing, in order to enable the engine to run happily on low-grade fuel. A litre of Silkolene's 'Pro Boost' octane boosting fuel additive is enough to last up to 1000 miles on low-grade fuel, assuming 50cc per gallon at 50mpg. Signs of an engine straining on poor fuel, known as detonation or 'pinking', are an apparent light tapping from the cylinder head, even under gentle throttle loads. Low power, overheating and feeling that your engine is about to destroy itself are also evident - this may well happen if the motor is pushed in power-sapping conditions.

Oil Coolers

An oil cooler is not an essential addition to your bike, unless you expect to be riding at either end of the cooler season. In this case, dry sump engines, i.e., those with separate oil tanks, lend themselves easily to this modification, as any of the external oil lines can be cut and a cooler with extra hosing spliced in. Fitting an oil cooler reduces the pressure and increases the capacity a little. However, having an oil cooler does not mean that important things like oil level, timing, valve clearances and carburetion can be neglected if the bike is to run well in hot and demanding conditions.

Fuel Filters

Whatever time of year you expect to be riding, it's worthwhile fitting an in–line fuel filter into the fuel line(s) of your bike. The translucent, paper element type works better than fine gauze, which most bikes have already inside the tank as part of the fuel tap assembly. Paper filters can be easily cleaned by flushing in a reverse direction with petrol from the tank In the Sahara, dust is always present in the air and even in fuel; you should guard against it at all times.

Clutch

If your bike has more than 20,000 hard miles on the clock, consider replacing the clutch plates before departure. In soft sand on a hot day it will be working hard and if it overheats and begins slipping , it may never recover. It is possible to squeeze a little more life out of a slipping wet clutch (as found on most singles but not on BMWs) by boiling the plates in detergent or preloading the springs with washers. Neither of these bodges can be expected to last long in the heat of the desert.

Vibration

If an engine had been removed at any time, or if you are riding one of the older singles which tend to vibrate (e.g., XT500 or DR400), a close eye should be kept on fittings, especially on home made racks, which can work loose over bumpy or corrugated terrain.

Air Filter

In the desert, dust is always a present and the air filter will require regular and possibly even daily cleaning during high winds. Make sure that the airbox lid seals correctly and that the rubber hoses on either side of the carburettor are in good condition and done up tightly at the clips. Greasing all surfaces inside the airbox is messy but catches more airborne particles and keeps the air filter cleaner for longer. To wash a re-usable foam filter (which are the best types to use) rinse it out in petrol a few times until the fuel appears clean, let it dry and then soak it in engine oil, *squeeze out the excess*, and reinstall.

Engine Oil

If using thicker 20/50 motor oil in your engine, as recommended for air-cooled bikes in hotter climates, take care to warm your engine up properly on freezing mornings, which you may experience at higher altitudes. This may require you blocking off the oil cooler or radiator (on a liquid cooler bike) until the engine is fully warmed up. In the Sahara it's not uncommon to experience a 25°C temperature variation in one day.

Conversely, when coming to a stop on a hot day, keep your engine running for a while, or do not turn it off at all if you are just checking your map. When you stop riding, the lack of airflow over the motor or through the radiator causes the oil temperature to rise momentarily. On air-cooled bikes, turning the engine off at this point causes the temperature to rise even more and it's not uncommon to notice a loss of power due to a slight seizure of the motor when starting up again. By keeping the engine running during brief stops on hot days the oil is kept pumping around, cooling the engine.

Chain and Sprockets

Shaft-drive systems are virtually maintenance-free forms of final transmission, enclosed from the elements. In this respect they are ideal for desert bikes, though they are usually fitted to heavier, more powerful machines, which bring about their own problems.

However, most trail bikes are fitted with more efficient (when correctly oiled and tensioned) roller chains and sprockets. Such an exposed system is prone to wear from sand, and lubricating an ordinary chain would immediately attract grit and accelerate the elongation of the chain and subsequent wear of the sprockets. Automatic chain oilers are a bad idea; they'll merely guarantee a sand–encrusted chain and although enclosed chain cases are an excellent idea, only MZ have managed to make a sufficiently robust item (but that's still not enough reason to go to the Sahara on an MZ!) – after market versions are only good for road riding and are horribly messy when it comes to changing wheels.

Standard and Self-lubricating chains

Running an ordinary chain dry in the desert causes it to overheat and tighten with possibly disastrous results for the transmission. 'Self lubricating' chains should not be confused with 'o' ring chains (see below). On these chains, the bushes are made of a metal impregnated with oil, but they last barely longer than an ordinary chain and still require regular oiling.

'O' ring chains

By far the best solution to this problem is to fit a good quality 'o' ring chain, such as those manufactured by DID, Izumi or Regina. These types of chains have a quantity of grease between the rollers and pins, sealed in with tiny rubber 'o' rings between the rollers and side plates. Only when these rubber seals finally begin to wear out after many thousands of miles (even in desert conditions) does the chain begin to wear out like an ordinary chain, hooking the sprockets as it goes. Oiling with a little engine oil, when appropriate, is only necessary on the sprocket-to-roller surface. Chain aerosol sprays are not needed. A DID chain fitted on a Yamaha Ténéré can last over 10,000 miles, with only half–a–dozen small adjustments needed in that time. Indeed DID's recent 'X' ring chain (effectively two 'o' rings with an additional grease reservoir in between) is guaranteed for 12,000 miles providing it's matched with good quality sprockets. For desert biking these types of chains are well worth the extra cost.

Sprockets

Good quality, hardened steel sprockets last much longer than lighter alloy ones. Beware of buying cheaper, pattern 'chain and sprocket kits' from some mail order suppliers who sell obscure brands of chains and inferior steel sprockets. Original equipment sprockets, i.e., those made by Honda, Yamaha, etc, are as good as any, especially when matched with a heavy duty 'o' ring chain. They are worth the extra expense for a longer service life.

Chain Tension

The chain should be adjusted to provide an inch and a half of slack, measured midway along the chain with your weight on the bike. On

A ratty honda XL250 in Djanet. The standard chain and Michelin T61s have worn out very quickly.

most trail bikes with long travel suspension, this will give an impression of an overly slack chain when the machine is unloaded and at rest, but this slack will be taken up once the suspension is compressed to the correct level when the bike is on the move. There will be a certain amount of tightening and polishing of the chain towards the end of a hot day. This will slacken off to the correct tension as the chain cools overnight.

Tyres

The choice of tyres is a difficult one to make for a long journey that may include thousands of miles of off–road riding. Basically, it boils down to long wear but poor grip on the piste from dual-purpose trail tyres, or faster wear on tarmac but better grip in the dirt from competition-oriented knobbly tyres.

In the end, the choice depends on your route, your riding style and your priorities. If you are 'just' crossing the Sahara, or continuing south to the Cape, then a trail tyre like the very long wearing Metzeler I or II Enduro, or their latest 'Sahara' version, might get you all the way with only a few punctures. The price of this longevity is vague steering, cornering and braking on any unconsolidated surface, at its worst in soft sand and mud. A better compromise, if you intend to spend some time off-road in the Sahara, is to ride down to the tarmac's end on a nearly worn-out trail or even a road tyre, and then fit a hard-wearing knobbly tyre for the piste.

Whichever tyre you choose, make sure it has at least four plies; anything less is designed for light unsprung weight and will not be resistant to punctures. For example, a front Metzeler Enduro I is especially flimsy, and has a tread pattern barely better than that of a road tyre.

Trail Tyres

Michelin T61s have quite a radical pattern for a trail tyre and would be suitable for use in the Sahara were it not for the fact that they wear so quickly. They may suit a lighter and less powerful machine like a Yamaha XT350. The Pirelli MT17 trail tyre would be a better choice for most 600s. It has the classic knobbly pattern of the T61 or Continental TKC90 (this being designated 70% off-road, 30% road use). However they are both still compromises, lacking the well-defined edges of a dedicated off-road tyre, such as a Metzeler Multicross knobbly, that makes cornering in the sand such a satisfying and predictable affair.

Knobbly tyres

Off-road competition tyres are made for a wide variety of track types. Choose a tyre designated for hard ground and rocks, not sand or mud tyres which may have a deeper tread but are made of a softer compound which will not last long at all when loaded up in the desert. For example choose a Dunlop K695 rather than a K990; or a Michelin AP10, not an MS10.

Knobbly tyres are designed to take a hammering off-road (admittedly on lighter, motocross bikes) and are generally sturdier than trail tyres. A front knobbly wears much less than a rear, and so it's possible to get away with a knobbly on the front and benefit from the better steering and braking off-road (but worse on tarmac). The rear trail tyre may slide around a bit but at least the front will stay put.

Michelin 'Desert' Tyres

Names like 'Sahara', 'Enduro', and percentage-use designations may only be marketing devices, but thankfully Michelin's 'Desert' tyre is the real thing, designed with 100% desert use in mind and used by probably the entire two-wheel contingent of the annual Paris-Dakar Rally. Riding on Michelin Deserts with heavy duty inner tubes (again, Desert tubes are available) and strong wheels is one of the best modifications you can make to your bike if you intend covering a high mileage off-road

The tread pattern resembles the T61 but there the similarity ends. These tyres were originally designed for heavy and powerful desert racers. Despite their notorious stiffness they can be fitted to most rims with ease, provided you use good tyre levers, plenty of lubricant and the right technique. This will probably be the last time you will have to use your tyre levers until the tyre wears out many thousands of miles later. Punctures with Michelin Desert tyres are extremely rare. These tyres can (and sometimes have to) be run virtually empty of air to allow the 'spreading out' necessary for optimum traction in soft sand. For the tyre's sake, speeds should be kept down in these circumstances.

Michelin Deserts have to be ordered from France through your local Michelin dealer. Allow up to eight weeks for delivery, or buy them in France on the way out, but note that around Rally time (December) they can be in short supply. A Desert tyre for the rear of a 600 single costs about £125, a bit less for a 21" front.

Tyre Creep

Besides causing the tyre to overheat, riding at the low pressures necessary for traction in soft sand can cause the tyre to creep around the rim. The inner tube is dragged along with the tyre as a result of braking and acceleration forces and eventually the valve will be ripped out, destroying the tube. Therefore, for low pressure use in sand it's essential to have security bolts fitted to both rims to limit excessive tyre creep. These devices clamp the bead of the tyre to the rim and may require a hole to be drilled in the rim. Keep an eye on your valves. If they begin to 'tilt over' it means that your security bolt may need tightening. Always keep the nut (usually 12mm) at the base of your valve loose or do not use it at all. Eliminating it allows more movement of the tube before the valve becomes damaged. These nuts are only useful as an aid to refitting tyres.

An alternative to security bolts, which can unbalance a wheel and get in the way when changing tyres, are self-tapping screws. These can be screwed through the rim so that they just bite the tyre, inhibiting slippage. Two each side of the rim set at 90° intervals should keep the tyre in place.

Punctures

Punctures are probably the most common breakdown you'll experience out there so practice wheel and tyre removal at home. This way when the inevitable event occurs in the desert you can be sure that the operation will be accomplished smoothly and without any trauma. Any emergency repair undertaken on the piste can be a little unnerving, especially when riding alone in a remote area. The better prepared you are to deal with these surprises the less you are likely to make absent–minded mistakes, such as forgetting to tighten a wheel nut or leaving your tools in the sand.

Among your spares you should include some washing up liquid (or liquid soap), talcum powder to sprinkle over a still–sticky repair, plenty of patches and rubber solution and, depending on your tyres' sturdiness, up to two spare inner tubes per wheel - especially if you intend riding in the sub-Saharan Sahel where thorn punctures are common. Also include a good pair of tyre levers, a pump from a mountain bike, a couple of spare connectors for the pump and a sliding-rod type air pressure gauge which is apparently the most accurate.

Rims built for tubeless tyres (which can and ought to be fitted with repairable inner tubes if riding in the Sahara) are designed to particularly fine tolerances and you may experience difficulty in fitting tyres and getting the bead onto the rim when inflating by hand.

Depending on the stiffness of the tyre and weight carried, 15 psi is the optimum all-round pressure to use off-road, 10 psi or less for soft sand, 20 psi or more on rocks. CO_2 cannisters may save some effort but the gas tends to leech out through the rubber. In the end there is no escaping a whole lot of pumping to repair a puncture. Avoid labour-saving aerosols like Finilec which are messy, unreliable and usually explode in your panniers anyway. The best way to repair a puncture is to fit a new tube without pinching it, though with some tyre and rim combinations this is easier said than done. Protect your pump from dust and loss; it is vital.

If for whatever reason you can't repair a puncture you can try stuffing the tyre with clothes or anything else that comes to hand (foliage, even if available, doesn't work, I've tried...) to regain its profile. If you do a good job you can carry on almost without noticing but if the tyre is damaged or starts to disintegrate you're better off dumping it and carrying on the rim – at a substantially reduced pace, naturally.

Wheels and Spokes

Modern trail bikes are built with light spoked alloy wheels to reduce unsprung weight and improve road performance. Some of the rims combined with thin spokes may not be up to the heavy beating they'll encounter over potholed tarmac and corrugated tracks. Unless you are competent at rebuilding wheels and tensioning spokes correctly, you can save yourself a lot of bother by fitting heavy duty spokes to your rim or, if necessary, uprating them altogether with quality rims (Akront are as good as they get), getting the work done by an accredited wheel builder. The benefit of having this work done is the difference between having to check and tension your standard wheels every evening, or ignoring the uprated items for the entire trip. To a certain extent, high tyre pressure and tough tyres protect rims from damage, so you should ride with the highest pressure for the terrain concerned.

It's not worth changing a trail bike's standard 21" front wheel for a 19" or 18" item for the sake of tube interchangeability, unless you are planning a long trip. The result is heavy steering and mixed up steering geometry, both of which are detrimental to off-road riding control. Excepting BMWs, the crucial odometer reading will also become inaccurate (see Navigation and Survival).

A small baggage fire within sight of Arlit, Niger

Petrol Tanks

One of the best features of the many 'rally replica' bikes is that they have large tanks, in some cases nearly enough to make the 400km run from Tamanrasset to In Guezzam on the trans–Saharan highway. Most bikes will, however, require at least 10 litres to be carried in reserve. For longer sections, across the Tanezrouft and between Djanet and Tamanrasset in Algeria, all bikes will require either a double sized fuel tank or a bulky 20 litre jerrican. In most cases even this will barely be enough.

Although a major expense, an enlarged tank holding up to 40 litres is preferable to taking up valuable space with full or empty jerricans. It places the great weight of a full tank in front of and below the rider, close to the machine's centre of gravity, thereby having a less pronounced effect on the balance of the bike.

A well constructed and sturdily supported tank with internal baffles can be built to hold up to 45 litres giving a range of up to 800 kilometres. Strong mountings and support are important, as such a tank adds up to 40kg to the weight of the bike when full. Tanks come in steel or plastic (nylon), and can be fabricated in Kevlar or, more cheaply in aluminium.

The Italian motocross equipment manufacturer, Acerbis, makes a number of large plastic tanks to fit most of today's popular trail bikes. They come in capacities from 20 litres to 45 litres, the latter made to fit the GS BMWs. This massive tank costs over £500 and can be made to fit other bikes too (e.g. the Suzuki DR350), although Acerbis's one-shape-fits-all "Africa" tank comes in a useful 30 litres size and costs a bearable £295. Despite their expense, plastic tanks combine the best in strength, lightness and durability, as well as providing resistance to vibration damage. They can also be easily repaired with epoxy glue should they develop a leak.

Aluminium is only popular in custom tank manufacture because it's soft and easy to fabricate into complex and attractive shapes that make the most of a bike's capacity needs. Its drawback is that it copes badly with vibration, either from the engine or from the terrain and the great weight of a full tank doesn't help in this instance. Cracks can be repaired with glue but aluminium welding facilities, requiring a much higher temperature than normal, are unknown in the Sahara. If you use an aluminium tank, be sure that it's well supported underneath, with heavy duty mounting plates locating it in place and pipe lagging around the frame's top tube to add support.

An inexpensive way of increasing your fuel capacity is to cram on a big tank from another bike and bashing it in the right places or, a messier and not always reliable alternative, enlarging the standard steel item by cutting and welding on additional sections or even an additional tank over the cut–down original. This latter method keeps the original mounting points but additional or strengthened mounts should be considered and any welding will, of course, have to be fuel tight

A neater alternative that still keeps the extra weight in the right place is to mount a pair of 10 litre jerricans, one each side of the tank, making sure there's enough clearance for your knees and the arc of the handlebars. This method may not do much for the bike's streamlining but does have the useful advantage of protecting your lower legs in the event of a crash. Jerricans can be surprisingly sturdy, but the rack you build for them should be strong enough to withstand these occasional spills or be easily repairable.

WHAT TO TAKE AND HOW TO CARRY IT

Suggested Equipment List

The list below is of the equipment taken for a planned two-bike trip around the Sahara covering about 5000 miles over a period of two months or so. We aimed to enable our bikes to cover about 500 miles between fill-ups while still keeping them rideable in the long stretches of soft sand expected in the northern Ténéré in Niger.

Deciding what to take will require a great deal of thought and planning. On a bike you don't have the capacity or ability to carry everything you would like to take with you. Despite this, overloaded bikes, however neatly arranged, are a common sight in the Sahara. Without being fanatical, you can really afford to take only the bare essentials with you if you want to keep your bike manageable off-road.

Everything in the following list fitted in the luggage bags, was attached to the bike, or was worn by the rider.

- **Luggage** Large Cordura holdall. Rucksack. Small tank bag. Canvas pouches on bashplate (for tools) near headlight and on rear rack (for water). Pair of home-made throw-overs holding a five litre container for fuel or water. A piece of 4" plastic drain-pipe was under the rack holding maps.

- **Sleeping** Full length karrimat. Caravan Quallofil three–season sleeping bag.

- **Cooking** Coleman Peak I petrol stove wrapped in tea towel. Lighter and matches. Rectangular army mess tins. Tin opener. Pan scrubber and small quantity of washing–up liquid. Swiss Army penknife. Plastic mug. Enough dried foods and beverages to last twenty days per person.

- **Washing** Bottle of liquid soap. Razor. Travel Wash concentrated detergent. Flannel. Small towel. Toothbrush and paste. Toilet paper.

- **Medicine** Anti–malaria pills. Multi-vitamins. Skin cream. Optrex. Lomotil. Rehydrat. Chapstick. Aspirin. Puritabs. Antiseptic cream and various dressings. Autan insect repellent.

- **Navigation** Silva type 15T compass. Michelin 953 map of North & West Africa. Map of France. IGN 1:1,000,000 maps of *Djanet, Bilma, Djado, Agadez, In Azaoua* and *Tamanrasset*. Various 1:200,000 photocopies of the Mt. Tiska, Seguedine and Bilma areas.

Some Ténéré Modifications

Tagasako rims replaced with DID rims and heavy duty spokes; Michelin Desert tyres and tubes fitted; fork springs preloaded with 1" spacers; rear shock removed and collar moved up to increase preload; front rubber brake hose replaced with stainless steel item from early Ténéré; handlebars and grips replaced with more comfortable items; seat repadded; DID 'o' ring chain and Yamaha sprockets fitted (a slightly longer chain had to be used to allow the large Desert tyre to clear the front of the swingarm); side stand foot enlarged; fuel filter fitted.

• **Clothing** (mostly worn while riding) Motocross boots. Kung Fu slippers (very compact!). 2 pairs of socks. Thermal underwear. 2 pairs of pants. 2 shirts. Woollen jumper. Tenson lightweight jacket. Rukka waterproof jacket Leather gloves. Damart thermal gloves. Leather trousers. Shorts. Woollen scarf. MDS MX helmet Scott goggles with spare dark and clear lenses. Kidney belt. (For more details see section on What to Wear, below.)

• **Bike Spares and Tools** 20 litre jerrican. Front and rear 'Desert' inner tubes. Michelin Desert rear tyre. Puncture repair kit. 2 connecting links for chain. CDI unit, control levers and cables (loaned by Mitsui). Oil filters and air filter. Spare ignition keys. Speedo cable. Gardening wire. Duct tape. Spare nuts, bolts and washers for rack fittings. Instant gasket. Araldite. Jubilee clips. Small tub of grease. Insulating tape. Electrical wire and connectors. Small G clamp. Spark plug. Petrol pipe. Bulbs. Lots of spare bungees and straps. Open/ring spanners in 8, 10, 12, 14, 17mm. Larger sockets and wrench, 10" adjustable spanner. Allen keys. Large and small, cross- and flat-bladed screwdrivers. Pliers with wire cutters. Feeler gauges. Bike manual with additional data. Spoke key. Tyre pressure gauge. Small hand-pump. Hacksaw with spare blades. Top-up oil.

• **Miscellaneous** Small Maglite torch. Compact 35mm camera with slide film. Ciné camera. Pen. Paper. Envelopes. Reading book. Documents and money. Spare batteries for camera and torch. French dictionary. Solar calculator. Mini rocket flares. Sixty second hand-held smoke flare. Candles.

Building Racks and Fitting Baggage

Once you've chosen and began preparing your bike, the question of how you are going to carry all your gear will soon crop up. Listed below are some considerations to help you decide:

• Convenient elasticated hooks won't be enough to guarantee a secure fitting. They are best backed up with 'Arno' type adjustable straps (available in various lengths from outdoor shops) to help secure the gear on your bike.

• The additional weight of hard luggage is worthwhile on a long trip where durability is an important factor. But note also that a metal boxed bike is a greater danger to the rider in the event of a crash and big boxes can get in the way when paddling in soft sand.

- Convenience of access, removal and security are important considerations too. Ideally, no item wants to be buried so as to discourage its use. For example, if your pump is at the bottom of your aluminium box, you may not bother returning your tyre to the correct pressure once you have regained a stretch of tarmac, which could later result in overheating and a puncture. Everything should be close at hand, and this is where large aluminium boxes with top lids often lose out. They should also be mounted so as not to impede wheel changes, either by offering enough room or by being easily demountable. One good thing about metal boxes, and probably the reason why most people fit them, is their relative resistance to theft.

- It is important to distribute all the weight as low and as centrally as possible. Light things like clothes, sleeping bags or empty containers can go on the back of the seat. It's best to regularly top–up the bike's tank from your jerrican to keep the weight of fuel in the ideal position. Paying close attention to the distribution of the weight of your baggage brings real benefits in the balance and control of your machine, as will be shown later.

Hard or Soft Luggage?

For a short trip (less than four weeks) or a trip where you do not expect to encounter bad weather or spend much time in cities (where

An early model Yamaha Ténéré loaded up for two, a burnt-out BMW having been abandoned in the dunes. Metzeler 'Enduro' tyres last for ages but give poor grip on the piste

most thefts occur) soft luggage will be adequate. On a longer trip or in the event of preference, hard luggage answers most needs while adding weight to the bike as well as time and expense to the whole endeavour.

If building or buying aluminium boxes, pad the contact areas with rubber or foam and sit the boxes on wooden bases to avoid chafing or annoying vibration. Bernd Tesch (see Useful Addresses), a German equipment supplier, also has bike boxes of 40 litres capacity for £70 and a sturdier version of 38/46 litres for £114/125. These latter ones are 2mm thick and are more suitable for off-road touring. They do not have the sharp corners that a home-made box might have, are good value for money and are popular with bikes in the Sahara. Tesch also sells racks for many trail bikes for around £180. Krauser-type panniers might look neat but are not up to the hammering they'll receive on the piste unless you substantially modify the mounting arrangements.

Instead, you can opt for soft luggage; throw-over panniers of PVC, Cordura (a hardwearing woven nylon), leather or canvas, with a rucksack on the back, a tank bag on the front, and other bags strapped on where they'll fit. It looks messy but it's light, cheap and versatile – it's also the least secure portage system. Throw-over panniers can stretch, melt, fall off, catch fire (if near the silencer), tear, disintegrate or simply get stolen. Indeed I have experienced all but the last of these problems in one eventful day! Some of these drawbacks can be overcome with careful thought and planning but you should bare these limitations in mind. However, soft luggage has a great advantage, in that you are unable to load it up with impunity as you might a metal box.

The popular throw-over panniers from Eurodesign and Swagman are cheap and capacious, but are not really up to the bouncing they will experience when fully loaded on the piste. They are bound to stretch, and they need some kind of support from beneath in the form of a light rack. Ex-army canvas panniers are cheaper still, and much more hard-wearing, but they don't always come in the size needed for desert touring.

Building a Rack

Another problem when using soft luggage without a rack is that by the time the bike is fully loaded up with, say a ten-litre fuel can on the back seat, the rear frame of the bike will flex, causing a weave at high-

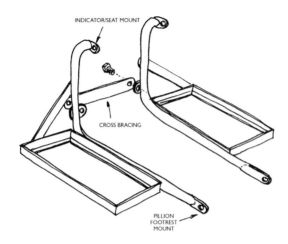

er speeds (over 50mph on the piste), especially when you have trail tyres fitted. The relative flimsiness of single-shock trail bike rear sub-frames (including GS BMWs) must be considered when load-ing–up luggage to ride off-road. M&P Accessories (see Useful Addresses) sell Riky frame stiffeners for most recommended desert bikes and which cure this deficiency while giving your luggage some support.

The minimum bracing necessary in this area is a box section or tube of mild steel from, roughly, the rider's footrests to the region of the rear indicators (when fitted), and this should be the basis of any rear carrier being built to carry boxes or bags. Based on this supportive beam, fur-ther struts can be fitted on to the pillion footrest mounts and at other convenient points in this region, which attach the carrier firmly to the bike's frame. A tray can then be welded to the rack to carry an alloy box, bags or a jerrican. These trays will need to be braced against inward flex-ing by a strut across the back, beneath the number plate or thereabouts. This strut must be far enough back so as not to interfere with the tyre on full compression of the shock, and it must be detachable to facilitate rear wheel repairs.

A rack should be bolted, not welded, to the bike's frame, using plen-ty of bolts, preferably all of the same size. Where appropriate it should leave room for the throw of the kick-start lever and in all cases the rack should leave room for the rider's calves when paddling for stability up a sandy river bed.

Testing Your System

It's essential to take your fully loaded bike out for a ride well before departure, with all tanks and cans full, to assess how it rides in this state, and to see whether the home–made rack makes contact with the swingarm or tyre during suspension movement. Sitting a friend on the back and getting them to jump up and down a bit is not the same thing! Riding your bike for the first time in this state will be quite alarming and you may wonder how on earth you are going to be able to manage it off-road, as you wobble up to the street corner. It may be your last chance to seriously re-assess your personal requirements and consider

Jerricans

Despite their awkward bulk jerricans are the simplest and cheapest method of safely increasing your fuel capacity. Original and serviceable wartime items can still be picked up at boot fairs for £5, although you should inspect the interior of any used jerrican for rust. Don't use a naked flame.

The standard jerrican (originally copied from a wartime German design, hence the name) holds 20 litres or 4.45 gallons when filled up in the upright position. This leaves an air gap just under the handles which should not be filled with fuel by tipping the can backwards unless you're really desperate. The air pocket, as well as the X-shaped indentations on the sides, enable expansion of fuel and bulging of the can. This relieves pressure on the rubber seal and so resists leaks. Because of this effervescent nature of petrol, a jerrican that has been shaken and warmed up on the back of your bike should be opened with extreme care. The clamp design of the lid makes this fairly easy. Suddenly opening an agitated jerrican full of petrol will result in a massive spurt of precious fuel.

The clamp-on spout (with an integral gauze filter and breather for smoother pouring) available from your local jerrican accessory outlet, is easier to use than a funnel and less wasteful than trying to pour the petrol straight in. You should also earth the container (drag it on the ground) before filling up your tank (especially if it has been carried on another vehicle) so as to disperse any static electricity that may have built up. Static is common in the dry conditions of the Sahara – see the chapter on Climate for a strange story.

The Far Eastern pattern copies, which are commonly available for around £14 new, are quite safe and reliable. Besides holding fluids jerricans make useful seats, pillows, small tables, props or 'centre stands' for wheel repairs. They're also a valuable and exchangeable commodity in the desert (as are the clamp-on spouts), often fetching higher prices than at home. Indeed they have become such a part of Saharan iconography that a Swiss adventure travel company has named itself Jerrican. Jerricans can be knocked about and dented for years while still remaining useful, but once rust or flaking paint begins to come out with the fuel a fine filter should be used or the thing discarded.

losing some weight somewhere. While it's loaded up, lay the bike over on its side. If you are unable to pick it up again, then it's too heavy, and you must reduce, or re-arrange, the weight.

Example of a Luggage System

On one trip, which was planned to be a two-month journey including a crossing of the Ténéré Desert, I took a lot of trouble in preparing my bike (an XT600ZE) and baggage system, basing it on the experience of my three previous desert trips.

A rack was built from steel tubing and strips, following the guidelines previously mentioned, using the two pillion footrest mounts at the front and tubes slotted into the frame ends at the rear (see illustration). One tray took a 20 litre jerrican on its side (jerricans need not be carried upright if the rubber seal is sound), while the other, slightly wider, tray accommodated a Cordura travel holdall which had its base reinforced with a 1/4" section of plywood. It located neatly into the tray and strapped down easily.

Long tyre levers and other heavy or bulky items were strapped down along the rack's sections with old bits of inner tube, or they were bolted on. Other bits and pieces, mostly spares, were stuffed into the bike's nooks and crannies so as to keep the main bag free from clutter and weight. A karrimat was strapped under the rack, but it dragged through bends and so was moved to the back of the rack. A rear Michelin Desert tyre took up this position until we reached the tarmac's end, where the worn-out trail tyre was discarded. Adjustable tie–downs held the tyre and jerrican in place. These strong straps (made to hold down racing bikes on trailers) are available from motocross shops.

On the back of the seat were slung a pair of home–made throw-overs from ex-army satchels which held a couple of five litre fuel containers (available at most garages or car accessory shops). These cheap and strong containers are ideal for either fuel or water. The throw-overs rested on top of the jerrican and Cordura bag, while on the seat was attached a rucksack containing clothing and a sleeping bag. A rucksack is always a handy thing to have for the odd occasion when you need to carry items yourself.

A thick canvas ammo pouch was bolted onto the front of the bash-plate and heavy tools were conveniently stored here. Ténéré tanks do not lend themselves to large, flat-based tankbags and so a small tankbag was used to keep important and valuable items in sight and readily avail-able. Another pouch near the headlight held a one-and-a-half litre water bottle for easy access. Two more water bottles were attached to the bike on the small rear carrier above the back light.

The bike had a capacity of 53 litres of fuel and 10 litres of water - the latter would have needed to be doubled had we reached the Ténéré Desert. The luggage layout gave instant access to most of the equipment and was straightforward to load–up in the mornings (when you can be absent-minded). The system was designed with convenience and centre of gravity in mind, and the risk of theft was minimised by one of us staying with the bikes when parked-up in towns.

Most significantly, the distribution of the weight was reflected in excellent handling considering how much was being carried (a maximum of about 65kg). The Ténéré was stable on the road and relatively agile on the piste, allowing challenging sections to be enjoyed rather than endured.

WHAT TO WEAR

WHEN RIDING YOUR BIKE in the desert you can expect to have to protect yourself against the wind, sun, heat, cold, dust and falling off. if you're unlucky you may experience all these things in one day. Your clothes should be practical, comfortable, warm and hard wearing, as you will probably end up wearing the same kit most of the time. For all garments, natural fibres and skins are preferable to synthetics, an exception being fibre pile garments like those by Helly Hanson or North Cape, which make very warm and light jackets or pullovers that dry quickly after washing.

Jackets and Trousers

A good jacket should not be too snug fitting and should have plenty of zipped pockets. Something like an enduro jacket works well but these are usually made out of nylon, which isn't an ideal material. Breathable and vented examples are ridiculously expensive but the freedom of movement they permit makes them preferable to an ordinary leather jacket. A jacket should seal up snugly around your neck, wrists and waist for cold mornings, being adjustable as the day warms up. Under a fairly loose jacket you can fit as many or as few layers as you want without feeling too 'stuffed' and unable to move easily on your bike. Look as your jacket as a kind of motorised *djellaba*, and sartorial briefcase, a practical and protective garment worn continuously and containing all your most valued items.

Winters in the Sahara are colder than expected, especially in the north, where you may be riding at higher speeds on tarmac, so a pair of overtrousers or long johns may be worthwhile. Mornings can also be very cold in the central mountains, but the lower speeds and greater effort exerted in riding on the piste will soon warm you up.

If there is one place in the world where waterproofs are superfluous it ought to be the Sahara but an unlined PVC jacket can make a useful ground sheet or provide an extra layer for those cold days in the north.

Boots

Invest in a proper pair of motocross boots to protect your feet and lower legs from injury. In a not infrequent low speed tumble in soft sand the rider can be pinned down by the bike and possibly burned by the exhaust pipe. The better you are prepared for these small accidents the more you will be able to enjoy your riding without fear of serious injury.

Gloves

Wearing a pair of padded palm motocross gloves is the most comfortable way to protect your hands on the piste while giving good feel at the 'bars, but you may find that Damart inner gloves, (useful at any time) or overmitts may be needed on the road. Fingerless cycling gloves are also cool and comfortable to wear when the weather and pace warms up.

Headwear

Eye, nose and ear complaints are common amongst the inhabitants of the Sahara and you should protect your eyes at all times when riding. Although all these matters are ones of personal taste and preference, a helmet which can accommodate a pair of motocross or ski goggles is most convenient. These light and comfortable goggles can be fitted with tinted lenses (illegal for road use in the UK) which will shield your sensitive eyes from sand, wind and glare much better than a full face helmet's visor, whether tinted or used with sunglasses underneath.

Riding without a helmet, while being very agreeable, is inviting sun stroke within a couple of hours in the Sahara. The least that will happen is that you will end the day with a splitting headache. Take a tip from the locals and always protect your head from long periods of strong sunlight, whatever the temperature is. A locally bought *cheche* (to give it but one of its many names), which is about six metres of thin cotton, will do the job perfectly, while making a voluminous scarf to wrap around your neck and lower face when riding but of course it won't protect your head in a crash. A *cheche* also makes an authentic souvenir of your trip.

Riding along in the desert will soon dry out your mouth and nose. By covering them with a scarf or *cheche* you'll keep them moist and so prevent cracked and bleeding lips and an itchy, runny nose irritated by dust. Lip salve works, but it tends to get covered in dust and grit.

Kidney Belts

Although some people find them uncomfortable, kidney belts will help support your back and keep you a little warmer on long tarmac days. A good belt (like those by Axo, the Italian manufacturers of motocross clothing) should have two velcro panels which can be adjusted to suit the contours of your waist. Avoid the cheaper, elasticated belts which simply clip together in an uncomfortable arrangement that digs into your stomach when you're riding. Kidney belts should be worn as tightly as feels comfortable - you will notice the difference at the end of a long day on the piste.

Body Armour

Whether to use full motocross body armour is really a question of riding style. By riding within your limits you need never come off at all, and indeed this should be one of your goals After just a few days of riding on the piste you'll find yourself slinging your heavily laden bike around with a certain casual aplomb, knowing just how far to push it. The very act of wearing protective body armour, can reduce your sensitivity to the dangers you are exposing yourself to, causing you to take unnecessary risks.

RIDING IN THE DESERT

ALTHOUGH RIDING YOUR BIKE through the desert isn't technically more demanding than negotiating a Welsh moorland bog, it's the remoteness and extremely long distances involved on a fully laden bike that can sometimes turn a small accident or breakdown into a perilous situation.

Do not compare riding in the desert with riding on a wide open beach, where you can bomb off at full speed without anything getting in your way. In the desert, riding this way will initially be a very exhilarating experience until you come across a rock, a soft patch or a shallow depression, indistinguishable in the midday glare at which time the lack of shadows make it difficult to judge perspective or distance. The front wheel gets deflected or digs in and you fly over the 'bars, closely followed by your cartwheeling machine. In this type of accident it's the bike that almost always causes the injury to the rider and on each of my trips I have come across, or heard about, riders who have come to grief in this way, with varying degrees of injury - broken collar bones being the most common.

Never take risks and always resist the impulse to show off. Travelling alone on the piste you will rarely feel like exceeding speeds of 50mph, and this will feel fast enough in the circumstances. At speeds greater than this it's not possible to react quickly enough to the ever–changing terrain. In the desert it's not so much the riding as the relentless concentration demanded by riding and navigating safely that will wear you out.

Ironically, although you will often be riding through spectacular scenery, the only chance you will have to fully appreciate its splendour is by stopping. While riding you will find yourself concentrating on the ground immediately ahead of you, looking for changes in colour or texture indicating softer or firmer sand (as a rule, the lighter the sand looks, the softer it is) or you might be moving across the track to find the shallowest corrugations. As stressed above, the ground ahead is always changing, demanding constant decisions and diversions.

RIDING IN SAND

Sand can be great fun to ride over if it's consistently firm, such as on a beach at low tide. In the Sahara, however, riding in sand requires a high degree of concentration: it can be extremely demanding to ride through sand if it's fine, or deeply rutted by other vehicles' tracks.

Riding in sandy *oueds* (dried up river beds) presents the most diffi-cult conditions that a biker regularly encounters. Here, fine water-borne sand is washed down by occasional rains, and if a track goes along a *oued*, rather than across it, you can find yourself riding in one of two 10" wide ruts for miles at a time. Very tiring! The key points here, and in all areas of soft sand, are:

• Low Tyre Pressures

By lessening the air pressure in your tyres to as little as 5psi, they flatten out and the 'footprint' your tyre creates on the sand lengthens significantly (rather than widens, contrary to the impression). Doing this changes your normally round tyre into more of a caterpillar track, increasing your con-tact patch and improving your traction dramatically. It can mean the dif-ference between getting across a sandy section or slithering around bare-ly in control, having to slow down only to get stuck or fall over.

In this severely under-inflated state a tyre gets much hotter, due to the internal friction created by the flexing carcass. Being soft and hot it's also much more prone to punctures. Never ride too far or fast on soft tyres, and be sure your security bolts or similar devices are done up tight as it's in low pressure/high traction situations when tyre creep can occur.

• Momentum and Acceleration

These are often the only things that will get you through a particularly soft stretch of sand, so don't be afraid to accelerate hard at the right time. A quick snap of the throttle in a middle gear will give you the req-uisite traction to blast across a short, sandy oued. A bike's handling and poise also sharpens up in this 'throttle on' condition. It can be hair-rais-ing stuff but this is often the only way to get through soft sand short of paddling along at 2mph or pushing.

• Standing up on the Footrests

While performing the above manoeuvre it's important to stand up on the footrests. Contrary to the impression that it raises your centre of gravity and makes you less stable, it does in fact have the opposite effect. It transfers your weight low, through the footrests, rather than through the saddle as when you are seated. This is why competition tri-als riders are always seen tackling tricky sections standing up on the pegs.

While standing up:
• your bike is much easier to control,
• your forward vision is improved
• you can better absorb shocks through your slightly bent knees

When you're standing up, grip the tank lightly between your knees to give your body added support and to prevent the bike from bouncing around between your legs. Padding on the inside of your knees or on the tank can help here

No matter how much your bike weaves and bucks around, keep the power on and stand up on the footrests for as long as it takes. It can be very tiring having to ride out long *oueds* or rutted pistes like this, but in most cases even trying to slow down and stop can mean falling over or getting stuck. For those keen to ride all the way to TImbuktu, note that the track north of the river from Bourem is like this for 200 miles.

Braking, Turning and Keeping Going

Braking and turning will demand greater care in soft sand. On unconsolidated ground it's best to avoid braking altogether and simply roll to a halt, otherwise the trench you dig might keep you there when you try to pull away. If this happens, hop off your bike and run alongside until it's moving freely without wheelspin, before jumping on again.

Change direction using your body weight rather than turning the handlebars and leaning. No matter how far the tread extends around the edge of your tyres, the best traction and the greatest stability is achieved with your bike as upright as possible. Make wide gradual turns wherever possible and if they tighten up, move your weight forward, being

Take it easy

Always ride within the limItations of:
• your vision
• the terrain
• your experience
• the bike's handling abilities
 and be aware of the consequences of
• an accident
• getting lost
• running out of fuel or water

prepared for the back wheel to step out, counteracted by a quick, supportive dab with your foot if necessary. Try and avoid sliding around, however, as there will be plenty of occasions when you get 'crossed-up' involuntarily without trying to do so for fun.

Sandy Ruts

About 20–25 miles an hour in third gear is the best speed to maintain when driving along sandy ruts, the low gear giving instant throttle response to further difficulties you may encounter. Slow down through the gears rather than with your brakes, and don't be reluctant to rev your engine hard should the situation demand it. This is when unreliable or ill-tuned engines begin to play up and overheat.

If you are in a deep rut, stay in it and don't try to cross ruts or ride out unless absolutely necessary. Again, on the Timbuktu piste, this can mean being ready to take a whack from an overhanging thorn branch. If stopping means falling off and you must change ruts urgently, hurl your bike and your weight in the preferred direction of travel while simultaneously giving a quick blast of power . . . but don't expect to get away with these kind of moves on a laden BMW with a passenger on the back.

On the Plain

Out on the sandy plain, try to cross other vehicles' tracks as close to right angles as is practical, so as to lessen the chance of your front wheel being deflected and bringing you down. 'Weight' the footrests as you do this by rising of the seat a little - it's not always necessary to stand right up. If transverse ruts become seriously churned up you may be better off trying to push your bike through or finding another way round.

Getting Stuck

Luckily, getting a bike stuck in the sand is nowhere near as big a problem as getting stuck in a car. The rider is usually able to extricate himself from the situation without assistance. You may have hit an unexpected soft patch in the wrong gear or at too slow a speed, and gradually your bike is dragged to a halt as you drop frantically through the gears. Do all you can to keep moving. Just before all forward motion stops, pull in the clutch so as to avoid futile wheelspin and, with the engine still running, hop off the bike and push while releasing the clutch, jumping back on once you're moving on firmer ground. This sort of activity is tiring and not something you want to do more than once a day, but keeping moving is the only answer to even more laborious digging, pushing and shoving.

Nevertheless sometimes you get caught. When the back wheel is buried up to the hub and the bottom of the engine is resting on the sand, stall the machine and turn off the engine. The bike will be standing up by itself at this point so turn off the fuel taps and lay the bike on its side. The rear wheel should now be hanging over the hole it excavated. Kick the sand back into the hole and pick the bike up again. The bottom of the engine should now be off the ground and the back wheel free. Lower the tyre pressures if you have not already done so, turn on the fuel and start the engine. An electric start helps enormously in these situations. With your engine running and your front wheel pointing straight ahead, let the clutch out slowly and push the bike forward. If the rear wheel begins spinning again, as may happen on an incline, stop immediately. Try and flatten the ground in front of the wheels so that they have no lip to roll over, and consider letting still more air out of the rear tyre even if it means you have to re-inflate it again as soon as you are free.

Also consider dragging your bike around so that it faces down the incline, from where it will start moving again much more easily. This may require removing your luggage. As a last resort, use your jacket under the back wheel as a sand mat to give you the initial bit of traction you need to get moving on to firmer ground. All the above procedures assume that there is no one else around to give you a helpful push.

Stuck in the sand – a rare occurence and not as bad as it looks.

Getting bogged down in sand is usually the result of limited experience, or of not reading the terrain correctly; of having too high tyre pressures or of revving your engine and spinning your wheels when you should have got off and pushed. As you become more experienced on the piste, these events should occur less and less, if at all.

Conclusion

Never let your concentration drop while riding in sand, even if it appears easy. Attack soft sections standing up on the footrests and with the power on. Maintain momentum at all costs, even if it means slithering around and riding in the totally wrong direction or jumping off your bike and running alongside, pushing it in first gear.

ROCKY MOUNTAIN TRACKS

In the Algerian Sahara, the rocky Fadnoun plateau and Eastern Hoggar tracks provide the type of consistent terrain where a well set up bike is at its best - being faster, easier and more enjoyable to ride than any other form of transport.

However, here the danger lies not only in damaging your wheels and getting punctures, but also in colliding with an oncoming supply lorry or riding off a cliff. Some rocky mountain sections demand reduced speed for no other reason than you cannot be sure what is around the next bend or over the brow of the hill. Keep your hands over the levers and be ready for anything: a grazing camel, a washed-out section of track following recent storms, holes, boulders, and, not least, a bunch of desert bikers parked-up, taking pictures of each other! Despatch riders will adapt well to the alert and anticipatory riding style required in the mountains.

Again, in the mountains, as much as anywhere, you must ride within the limits of your visibility and the terrain. Read the ground constantly. A steep descent may end up in a sandy *oued* or wash-out, while a steep ascent rarely continues down in the same direction. After just a few hours of this you will find your judgement and reflexes improving noticeably.

Try and ride your bike 'light' over rocky country. By not being tense and gripping the bike too firmly you are able to preserve both yourself and your bike from sudden and tiring shocks, absorbing and neutralising them instead of resisting them with tensed muscles and clenched teeth. As on sand, weight the footrests over any cross ridges or V-shaped dips.

You will find that this kind of responsive riding saves both physical and mental energy during the course of a long day on the piste.

One good thing about tracks in the mountains, as opposed to those on the plain, is that they are usually well formed, and navigation presents little difficulty, providing you know what crossroads or forks are coming up ahead. This isn't always so clear, so refer to your map and trip odometer.

Corrugations and Berms

Corrugations, the regular washboard surface which an unconsolidated track develops, occur on all pistes in the Sahara where lots of vehicles are confined to one route. The easier route from Tamanrasset up to Assekrem in the Hoggar is well known for its horrible corrugations, made worse by the impossibility of riding on the boulder-strewn terrain on either side. There are many explanations for the presence of these infuriating formations, such as the braking and accelerating forces of passing traffic, pulsating shock absorbers or the bouncing of heavy trucks - but, like the mystery of sand dunes, none of these seem really adequate.

In a car, you have to grit your teeth and pray that the shock absorbers and other suffering components will survive. The best solution is to accelerate up to about 40 or 50 mph and skim across the top of each ripple, so that the vibration is reduced dramatically. On a bike, the same practice can give a smoother ride too, but at this speed your wheels are barely in touch with the ground and your traction is negligible. In a straight line this is not too dangerous, but on a bend it's possible to ride right off the track. On a single track vehicle like a bike you only have a few inches width to worry about and you may find that corrugations may be shallowest or non existent right on either edge of the track, but not for more than a few metres at a time. You will always be weaving around trying to find the smoothest path

If possible avoid the corrugated piste altogether. For example, the spectacular 130km piste from Bordj El Haouas to Djanet in south-eastern Algeria is corrugated for its entire length. In French colonial days it used to be sealed and barely discernible sections of tarmac still remain at the eastern end. The heavily-laden trucks that keep the isolated oasis of Djanet supplied keep those corrugations in good shape, as they are unable to drive on the soft sand either side of the track. However, on a bike with significantly reduced tyre pressures you can ride all the way to Djanet and back in far greater comfort and freedom off the piste, taking time to explore the creeks and canyons of the Tassili cliffs to the north, or the dunes of the Erg Admer to the south.

Corrugations do however, have one small saving grace. A very easy place to get lost anywhere in the world is near a settlement, be it a capital city or African village. Near a desert settlement there may be many minor tracks leading to places connected with the village and the main route might go right through the village or bypass it altogether. Generally, in the desert, the most corrugated track is the one most frequently used by vehicles passing through and the one you will most likely want to follow. There may even be times out on the plain when you are a little lost, that the sight and feel of corrugations will be an immense relief, signifying that you have relocated the major track from which you inadvertently strayed.

On fast bends, 'berms' (the built-up edge of the track) can be used to ride around the bend much faster and more safely than you could do on flat ground. In effect, by riding around the bank, the ground is leaning 'up' at you rather than you having to lay your bike 'over' and so berms can be ridden at alarmingly high speeds fairly safely. This is not the advanced motocross technique that it may seem, as your angles of lean are not too radical. Rather, it's a way of riding out bends without having to resort to tiring (for yourself) and inefficient (for your bike) braking and acceleration. 'Berm bashing', when you get it just right, is also a whole lot of fun!

ROAD RIDING

Even road riding in the Sahara is not as straightforward as it might seem. Three hazards exist that should all be treated with caution: camels; potholes (sometimes wider than the road itself) and sand.

• Camels on the Road

You can expect to find a camel anywhere in the desert, despite the fact that they all belong to someone and the owner knows more or less where they are. For some reason these beasts are attracted to the tarmac possibly, like kangaroos in Australia, because of the heat the tarmac retains at the end of the day as temperatures drop. Whatever the time of day, if you see camels on or near the road, slow down and be ready to brake hard. Do not expect them to scatter at the sight and sound of your scooter. On the contrary, you can expect the most illogical and erratic behaviour from them, and from all other domesticated beasts you'll come across in Africa. A camel may run across the road out of your way and then suddenly turn back across your path and cause a col-

lision. It may be grazing peacefully by the roadside and then be so startled at the sight of you that it runs straight at you. Ride very carefully
when passing close to camels and be ready for anything.

• Potholes

A few years ago, most of the road south of El Golea (now called El
Meniaa) to Tamanrasset was in a terrible state. Potholed and broken up
by passing traffic on the Tademait plateau; undermined by flash floods in
the Arak Gorge and degenerated completely to corrugated track as it
neared Tamanrasset. One memorable section of tarmac consisted of a
100 foot-wide chasm, with 25 foot sides, appearing like a ravine waiting
to be bridged. In fact this enormous quantity of material had been
washed away by the desert storms of 1981-2.

Legend has it that there was only one year, in the late 1970s, when
you could drive the entire distance from Algiers to Tam, about 2000km,
in a fast car in one very long day. Now it might be more like three, if you
are in a hurry. A couple of years ago it would have taken even longer.
The rebuilding of the trans–Sahara highway has occupied the army for
many years, and maintaining it probably guarantees all the conscripts
jobs for life. The tremendous temperature the tarmac reaches (in summer it may be close to boiling point), as well as the passing of heavy-
weight traffic, ensures that as soon as one section is repaired another
begins to deteriorate.

Once one pothole appears you can be sure that there will be more
ahead. You have to concentrate hard in these sections, as the mindless
routine you have been used to on the smooth, empty highway is soon
disrupted by hard braking, swerving and optimistic acceleration. A pothole's sharp edges can easily put a dent in a wheel rim at 40mph and you
must be prepared to manoeuvre to avoid this.

Luckily, on a bike, unlike in a car, you are able to squeeze through
tyre-width sections of solid tarmac where two holes are about to meet.
Generally, because of your single track and greater manoeuvrability, you
will have an easier time on corrugations than cars will. In the end, of
course you always have the option of riding on the desert floor on
either side of the road, which may be slower going but will prove more
consistent than a badly damaged road.

• Encroaching Sand

The final common hazard on the tarmac highway is at places where
dunes are encroaching, or where wind has deposited tongues of sand

across the road. There are certain areas on the trans–Sahara highway where this is always the case, and the triangular warning signs with 'SABLE' (sand) written underneath should be heeded. One such place is on a rise north of El Golea - the sand here is occasionally removed by a plough, but the dangerous combination of a bend at the top of a rise is repeated elsewhere along the highway.

Immediately north of In Salah and, again, a few miles further south of it, the dunes that are slowly moving across the road are easily spotted, and are either driven round or driven through. Two ruts such as you would find across a *oued* have usually been formed by passing traffic and to ride through successfully you must balance speed with caution.

Although it's momentum that gets you through soft sand like this, riding into these sandy ruts at highway speeds will almost certainly knock you off. The sudden build-up of sand in front of the front wheel will dramatically alter the 'castor' effect of the steering and flip the wheel sideways, sending you head-first into the sand. Don't expect a soft landing either. On one occasion at the southern In Salah dune, I came across

Coming off the Fadnoun plateau near Zaouatallaz, Algeria.
See route D.

a rider from an organised tour group who had broken his leg trying to blast through the ruts. What he may have failed to do, was to slow right down to about 25–30 mph, drop a couple of gears and then accelerate as fast as necessary, while standing on the footrests. In this mode, the poise of the bike becomes more stable and predictable; the front wheel is lightened and the rear wheel slithers around, but if you stay in the rut you will make it back onto the tarmac, just in time to enjoy the adrenaline rush - for as with all these tricky manoeuvres, getting them right is satisfying, a relief, and great fun.

NAVIGATION AND SURVIVAL

NAVIGATION IN THE SAHARA does not, as many people assume, involve riding across the dunes on a compass bearing. More often than not you will be riding along a clearly defined track guided by occasional cairns, marker posts (known as *balises*) or old oil drums (*bidons*) buried in the sand. As long as you keep these in sight and ride close to the main piste you will be on the correct route.

At times the piste may not be clearly defined, such as across the sandy plain on the way down to In Guezzam south of Tamanrasset, where the 'track' may be several miles wide as the traffic weaves around for the smoothest and firmest terrain. Even here the orientation of the route is clearly north-south and the tracks converge around the Laouni dunes, where corrugations restart as the traffic is funnelled down past the Gara Eker escarpment.

Elementary Orientation

Navigation anywhere requires knowledge of where you are as much as where you are going. Even on the tarmac highway, where distances between settlements are vast, you should always take the trouble to know your position as accurately as possible. When on the piste, landmarks such as major *oued* crossings, distinctive mountains or steep passes should be reassuringly anticipated with regular reference to your map, odometer and guidebook or route notes. For example at a major junction the map indicates a distinct turn to the south where the route enters a narrow valley about 70km ahead. Add 70 to your odometer reading and repeat the total figure "valley – south – xkm" a couple of times. As the "xkm" reading rolls up on your trip you should be ready to turn south allowing a bit of slack for your rough estimate.

In fact, on a long route of several hundred kilometres it's a good idea to note down the details of the complete itinerary such as distances, landmarks, wells, and stick them to your handlebars or tank bag for easy reference as you ride along. Estimate your total fuel range (how far you can go on your tank, jerricans, etc) conservatively and note down the

CIRCULATION OF TOURISTS' VEHICULES ACROSS THE GREAT SOUTH

The wali of Tamanrasset communicates:

Tourists travelling across the **Great South** are asked to conform to the legal prescriptions in vigour :

● To drive on the roads classified «**B**» In Amguel-**Zaouia** El kahla- Amguid - In Ekker-Tamanrasset - In Guezzam - In Amguid tourists should, OBLIGATORY solicit the civil protection service of the district (witaya) of Tamanrasset, for a journey authorization ●

● The roads classified «**C**» are very dangerous to be used, tourists should be aware of that ●

   ● **IN SALAH - AMGUID**
   ● **TAMANRASSET - IN AZZOUA**
   ● **TAMANRASSET - TINZAOUATINE** ●

Besides, it recommended to tourists :

● To drive robuste vehicules in perfect state, well equiped with special tires for these particular roads and a filter against sand (oil bath).

● To drive in day-light and in groups of at least, two vehicules ●

● To have an extra food of two days in addition to their need, a reserve of fuel, a medical first aid case and a sufficient reserve of drinkable water ●

● Never leave the main road and in case of breakdown, never get far from the vehicules ●

● Before setting out your journey, it's wise to consult the authorities of the security services for information about the conditions of the roads ●

It's vividly advised to tourists to avoid crossing the Great South in the estival season that's from june **1**st until **september 15**th and that's because of the high temperature and windstormes ●

Warning sign south of Tamanrasset.

mileage reading at which you expect to run out, ensuring that it's well over the total distance to the next fuel point.

Zero your trip odometer at the beginning of a stage when all your reserves have been replenished, and only reset it again at your next safe destination or when you refuel your tank. The resettable 'trip' is a far more useful instrument than your speedometer needle and is why a spare speedo cable should be carried amongst your essential spares. It tells you how far you have travelled, and therefore acts as a guide to your position and, crucially, your remaining reserves of fuel.

For quick checks on your orientation (which direction you're travelling in: southeast, west-northwest, etc) it's easier to use the sun rather than referring to your compass, which requires stopping to get away from the bike's magnetic influence – at least 10 metres. The fine degrees of accuracy a compass can offer are not usually necessary for ordinary desert bike navigation. In the northern hemisphere, the sun always travels left to right throughout the day. Always keep half an eye out for the sun and get to know the directions of the shadows at various times of the day. After a while, a quick glance at your shadow and your watch will instantly tell you whether you are riding in the right direction for your section of the route.

All these precautions as designed to mitigate the mild apprehension of riding out into the wilderness for a few days. Knowing, or trying to anticipate what lies ahead and being broadly right is most gratifying and gives you confidence that you're going to make it to the other end safely. Blindly following tracks without giving a thought to landmarks, orientation or maps is the most common way of getting lost. Sometimes a track can inexplicably begin to turn the wrong way or peter out altogether. If you are tired, low on fuel or your bike is running badly, these moments of uncertainty can lead to careless decisions such as trying to take a short cut back to your last known position. Off-piste, in mixed terrain, getting totally disorientated is as easy as falling off your bike; and if you are pinned down by your bike just a mile off the piste, but out of sight, you may never be found. If you lose the main piste, or following a night spent some distance away from the main route, always follow your tracks back to the point where you left the piste, or near enough. Correcting these sort of mistakes is where a bike's barely adequate fuel reserves are often used up.

If you are ever in doubt, don't hesitate to stop and think – don't carry on regardless hoping that things will work themselves out. Look around you and consult your map, compass and odometer carefully. Look out for any *balises*, traces of corrugated track or any other clues as to where you might be. If you are lucky enough to have a major land-mark such as a distinctive peak which is marked on your map, take a bearing to help narrow down your position. It's a rare luxury to have two such landmarks but if they are sufficiently far apart, you can accu-rately triangulate your position and you are no longer lost. If these basic navigation techniques are unfamiliar to you, learn them before you leave, it'll take a couple of hours at most. Outdoor sports shops should sell elementary orienteering guide books such as the *Ouward Bounds Map and Compass Handbook* (£7.99) which will explain exactly how to take a bearing and how to plot your position on a map. In the Sahara there is rarely an alternative piste leading to a different destination that you do not know about, but do not discount this possibility.

Riding in a Group

Getting completely lost on the main piste is rare, but losing sight of your riding companions is more common. Before you set out on an unknown section, clear rules and signals should be established. When travelling in a convoy with other tourists in cars the pace is usually slower and a bike generally has no difficulty keeping up.

Out on the open plain, bikes can ride within sight of each other side by side, but if riding in line on narrow tracks one rider should take the lead and keep it, glancing back occasionally for his companions. If the group is of mixed riding ability then it's best for the slowest rider to lead, even if it becomes frustrating for the hotshots who have to eat their dust. The simplest signal should be flashing headlights - "I am slowing down or stopping" - and on seeing this the leader should stop and wait or turn back if necessary. For this reason it's worth retaining at least one of your rear view mirrors.

A common way to lose each other is when the leader stops to wait for the follower to catch up. After a while of waiting and wondering, the leader retraces his route to look for the other rider. In the meantime the following rider, having seen the lead rider struggle through some soft sand (for example), has taken another route around a hill and races ahead to catch the leader, who by now is inexplicably out of sight. Rider number two races ahead to catch the leader who is in fact behind him, meander-ing searchingly in the opposite direction. It is the responsibility of all rid-ers to look out for each other - this should stop any arguments as to whose fault it is. The leader should slow down or stop if he gets too far ahead of the rest of the group, who in turn should never stray too wide-ly from the route.

If you do lose sight of each other, ride to some high ground, turn off your engine, look around and listen for the others. In this position, you are also more likely to be seen by the rest of the group, and hopefully you'll catch sight of each other, hands shading your brows, on neighbouring hills. Failing this, an agreed procedure should be strictly adhered to. For example after a certain agreed time apart, you should all return to the point where you last stopped or spoke together. If fuel is critical then you should stop ahead at a clear landmark, such as a village or junction.

The whole point of riding together is to give each other much needed moral support during a clearly risky endeavour, so resist any individualistic tendencies and stick together while traversing remote pistes.

Riding Off-Piste

Unless you know exactly what you are letting yourself in for and where you are going, navigation off-piste is beyond the capabilities of unsupported motorbikes, with their limited provisions and narrow margins of safety. You might look at the Michelin 953 map and think for example, it would be interesting to cross totally virgin desert to a parallel road or track 200km to the west or explore that remote range of mountains. While this might seem like a laudably adventurous idea when the map is spread out on the kitchen table, in reality it's extremely risky for all but the best, well-equipped and most experienced riders.

The reason why pistes have developed along the lines that they have over the millennia is that they take the line of least resistance between oases and wells in a landscape and environment hostile to all travel and life. For the beginner, these pistes offer enough of a challenge in themselves. Away from the piste, even a small gorge or ridge of hills can mean a disorientating detour, or provoke an attempt to ride across terrain that uses up lots of fuel and the rider's energy, resulting in a crash.

If you're into this type of extreme adventuring you're much better of doing it as part of an expedition including 4WDs to carry the essential reserves fuel and water. Bare in mind also the wisdom and safety of riding into unvisited terrain, especially near sensitive border areas (which includes just about all border areas in Africa). Bored army patrols or trigger-happy smugglers might be delighted to see you – but not for reasons you'd care to mention.

Navigation techniques

Riding off-piste alone on a bike isn't recommended, but if you think you know what you're doing then navigation is something you'll have to consider seriously. Below are three elementary navigation techniques and as you'll see, satellite navigation is clearly the best suited to desert biking in remote areas.

Dead Reckoning

The technique of navigation known as dead reckoning - plotting a theoretical course on a map and following it using accurate distances, bearings and possible landmarks - requires a full time navigator concentrating solely on orientation and so is beyond the scope of solo desert biking.

Dead reckoning assumes that by travelling 10 miles north (0°), 10 miles southeast (120°) and ten miles southwest (240°), you should return to the point from where you began, having ridden in a large, equilateral triangle. However, reading a compass accurately while riding a bike is impossible, and even the slightest error in calculation becomes magnified over distance. Just a 1° error to the west (359° instead of 0°) along the first third of the route would return you a couple of miles from your starting position. If you are searching for a specific point, such as a vital well, this distance could mean the difference between finding it and just missing it.

Satellite Navigation

The advent of inexpensive hand-held GPS (Global Positioning System) receivers now means that you don't need the financial resources of a major expedition to get the equipment to locate yourself precisely, anywhere in the world. They're unnecessary for most adventurous motorcycling in the desert, but are at least are now within reach of the dedicated amateur two-wheel explorer.

Operated and maintained by the US Department of Defense and developed as part of Star Wars programme, some aircraft deployed GPS-guided missiles during the Gulf War. Even since that time the System has improved with the full constellation of two dozen satellites now spinning around the globe enabling speedy

The Philips PHN101, Magellan Meridian and Garmin GPS45
hand-held GPS receivers

and precise fixes. Depending on the position of three or more of these
satellites at a given time, you can get a position accurate to within 100
metres anywhere on Earth in about fifteen minutes and updated fixes in
a couple of minutes. Were it not for the degradation built into the signal for civilian use, (called Selective Availability but correctable with
additional gadgetry), worldwide accuracy to within a couple of metres
would be possible, but in the desert, 100 metres is pretty handy. To
receive a good signal you need to be out in the open, fairly easily
achieved in the Sahara, but bare in mind that securing a fix in a deep
canyon may be not possible if the available satellites are low on the horizon.

Fixes are given on an LCD readout in latitude and longitude
(degrees, minutes – a sixtieth of a degree, and seconds – a sixtieth of a
minute. The distance between two seconds on the earth's surface is one
nautical mile or 1.85km). You then transpose this information onto your
map and that's were you are. Ideally you should have known that before
you took your fix, but on land, the comfort of confirmation that GPS
offers is what it's all about. If you're off course you can then plot a
course towards your destination.

Some receivers have a 'waymark' facility for plotting complicated
routes; more useful for zig-zagging through reefs into a harbour and difficult to use while riding as well as wearing down the batteries through

continuous use. Expensive models can have a host of additional advanced features such as ground speed, graphic map screens and ETA at your given destination, but for desert biking off piste it's the most basic position-fixing facility which will be most useful.

A hand held GPS receiver about the size of last year's mobile telephone now costs less than £350. Models to consider in this price range include the Magellan Meridian, Garmin GPS45 and Philips PHN 101. See Useful Addresses for details of suppliers but remember using GPS can guide you accurately and reliably to places beyond your dreams - as well as places beyond help should you break down. They must be seen as merely an aid, albeit an outstanding one, to navigation. You still must be competent with the reading and interpretation of maps (which may not necessarily match your receiver's accuracy), taking bearings and plotting routes. Their proper use is recommended only for experienced groups, ideally with a support vehicle carrying extra water, fuel and spares. Inquisitive or envious border guards may also take an interest in your handy little GPS receiver and confiscate it; it's probably a good idea to disguise, disable or better still, conceal it at these times.

Astral Navigation

This archaic system of navigation which enabled Da Gama and Cook to make their discoveries has now been thoroughly eclipsed by GPS. Astral navigation is a time consuming task fraught with the potential for human error. It requires a sound knowledge of the stars and an accurate sextant, an even more accurate watch (or shortwave radio), tables, protractors and, of course, maps. Much time and possible miscalculation can be saved by using a pre-programmed computer/calculator to take the place of the tables. Such a system is not necessary on the main pistes and should only be considered as a means of navigation off-piste by those already very familiar with taking astral readings.

When Things Go Wrong

Compared to cars, motorbikes are fairly reliable by virtue of their simplicity. Water-cooling systems are well tucked in and electronic ignition either works or it doesn't. The most likely cause of immobility is running out of fuel, for whatever reason. If this happens obviously there is nothing you can do until someone offers you some fuel or a lift to get some. On the main pistes in winter you should not have to wait for more than a few hours. Nevertheless, have signals ready to make it clear that you need assistance because, on a wide piste other vehicles may not pass close enough to see you. If someone offers you a lift, leave a timed

Emergency Equipment

- Lighter or matches – for fire or signalling
- Aluminium space blanket or bag – for daytime shade and nighttime warmth
- High-energy compact rations, including salt
- Rescue flares – hand held smoke or rocket type Only use your rocket flares when you are certain they will be seen by potential rescuers.
- Compass and map
- Torch
- All the water you can carry

message on your bike explaining your actions and don't leave anything on it that you expect to see again, including the bike.

On the main piste help should arrive fairly quickly, but if you have strayed from the main piste, or you are lost and alone with an immobile bike, you must now face the fact that you are in serious trouble. Once you have done all you can, and are certain that your machine will not run, your next priority is to attempt to assess your position as accurately as possible and to ascertain your water supplies.

If you have been regularly referring to your map, odometer and any landmarks then your position can be estimated fairly accurately. If you are certain that no one will come this way - i.e.. you are way off-piste with no tracks but your own - then you must be prepared to walk back to your last known position on the piste. If broken down on the piste, staying with your vehicle makes sense, as your chances of being seen and surviving for longer are far greater, but no one is going to be searching for you off-piste.

Walking Out

As soon as you begin walking in the desert your water consumption will increase dramatically. Even on firm ground you are unlikely to average more than two miles per hour. If you have more than a few miles to walk, you are better waiting till evening or early morning, when the lower temperatures and marginally firmer ground make distance-walking less tiring. Before you leave, have one last look around from some high ground. There may be a nomad encampment nearby.

You should carry as little as possible, wear light and comfortable clothing and, most importantly, cover your head against the sun during the day and the cold at night. The first four items listed in the box above are best wrapped up in duct tape and stored in a secure place amongst your kit, hopefully never to be needed. Most of this equipment could fit in your pocket. To carry water, a harness should be made up to support this heavy weight on your back – your rucksack may now be useful. Follow your tracks religiously and avoid short cuts and/or steep ascents unless you are certain they are worthwhile. Conserve energy and so, water, at all costs.

Walking out should not be considered lightly, it's a last resort to save yourself when all else has failed. Attempt it only if you are certain as you can be that your machine is beyond repair and no one will come your way. A situation like this need not happen if you ride with others or stick to known, regularly used pistes.

Looking Out for Others

In remote Saharan towns it may be necessary to check out with the police and fill in various cards "*pour votre securite*", giving details of your party and destination. Indeed, at the petrol station in Djanet, southern Algeria, they ask to see these papers before they will fill up your tank. However, the authorities in Algeria have long since abandoned expensive searches for the growing bands of missing tourists in their part of the Sahara. The most they might do is to ask an arriving party whether they have noticed a couple of missing vehicles that are a week overdue. People get lost and disappear on the clearest of pistes in conditions of perfect visibility.

As a traveller in the Sahara you have a responsibility to others, whether tourists or locals, so don't just pass by with a wave when you see a bunch of people gathered around a steaming radiator or an ill-equipped car stuck in the sand. An extra shove from a passing biker may be all that they need to get moving again. You will get used to people stopping and enquiring with a quick "Ca va?" when you are parked up by the side of the road. You should be reassured by this courtesy but, if it begins to irritate you (as it may do after a while) then park away from the road, where exchanged waves are an accepted signal of all being well.

A Few Final Tips

In the Sahara, three things will ensure that you of reach your next destination safely:

• **A reliable and well equipped bike**

• **As much fuel and water as you can carry for the route**

• **Common sense.**

RULES OF SURVIVAL

The following rules will help ensure your well-being in the desert. They are not in any strict order of importance.

NEVER TAKE CHANCES. Keep on the piste, carry adequate reserves of fuel and water and ride within your limitations.

DON'T WASTE WATER. Get in the habit of being miserly with your washing and cleaning needs, but drink as much as you need.

INSPECT YOUR BIKE DAILY. Oil level, wheels and home-made components may need regular attention.

CARRY ENOUGH FUEL AND WATER FOR YOUR ENTIRE PLANNED ROUTE. Recognise that difficult terrain and maximum loading may increase your consumption of these vital fluids.

CARRY ESSENTIAL SPARES AND TOOLS. And know how to use them. You should at least be familiar with tyre removal and repair, oil and air filter changes and fault diagnosis.

KNOW WHERE YOU ARE AND NEVER CARRY ON WHEN LOST. Stop before you go too far, accept that you have made an error, and retrace your steps if necessary.

IF YOU CHECK OUT ON DEPARTURE, CHECK IN ON ARRIVAL. This may take some perseverance, as the authorities can appear indifferent, but it is an essential courtesy that may prevent wasted searches later.

KEEP YOUR COMPANIONS IN SIGHT AT ALL TIMES. Or tell them what you are doing and where you are going.

NEVER DRIVE ON THE PISTE AT NIGHT. Even on the tarmac roads in Africa there is always a danger of unlit vehicles, stray animals and potholes.

The fact that you are in a potentially perilous situation does not need underlining. Your decisions and the way you conduct yourself will be fundamental to your survival.

Riding and navigating in the desert require a clear thinking mind aware of its own fallibility. As Tom Sheppard notes in his E.A.C. report, Desert Expeditions, published for the Royal Geographical Society;

> *"Nothing compares to the alarm and sinking feeling of knowing something has gone wrong with the navigation."*

It is very rare that you will become completely lost. More likely you will be, in the words of the time-worn adage "temporarily unaware of your whereabouts". You must use your logic and common sense to work out where you went wrong, and correct your mistake sooner rather than later.

Take compass bearings away from the magnetic influence of your bike. A pair of mini binoculars can be useful when looking for lost companions or distant *balises* obscured by the wind-blown haze. Competent orientation that excludes hasty judgements will inspire confidence and a feeling of security in a situation which is always slightly tense.

WATER

AS YOU MIGHT EXPECT, WATER is a big issue in the Sahara. Even in the depths of a north Saharan winter you'll soon become aware of the heat, and especially the dry air, once you begin to do something strenuous, like trying to jump-start a recalcitrant bike up a sandy oued or perhaps just walking up a dune. After such exertion you'll feel the need to take a healthy swig from your water bottle.

At the coolest time of year a 10 litre water container, plus a 1.5 litre water bottle kept conveniently at hand would be the bare minimum to last you the leisurely three-day trip between Tamanrasset and Djanet. This quantity is for drinking and cooking only, and leaves you with barely adequate reserves of just a few litres.

On a less busy route, such as the 700km run to Bordj Moktar from Tamanrasset (being out of the highlands this route is appreciably warmer) more water should be carried, or a visit planned to the well at Tlm Missao. A water bottle wrapped in a damp cloth will become much cooler through evapotation and so make a refreshing drink during hot weather.

In the very end, when everything else has broken down, run out or fallen off, it is your water that will keep you alive. Be sure to attach your water containers securely to your bike and check regularly that they, and the rest of your baggage are still attached and intact, particularly over rough ground or following a heavy crash.

Water and the Human Body

The average person, weighing around 70kg, is made up of 50 litres (50 kg) of water. Even if just a small percentage of this water volume is lost through sweating urination or vomiting, and is not replenished, the average person will soon begin to experience the some of the following symptoms:

Water lost	up to	Symptoms
5%	(2.5 litres)	Thirst, vague discomfort, lack of appetite, sickness, irritability, sleepiness.
10%	(5 litres)	Dimness, headaches, difficulty in breathing, stum bling, slurring, lack of saliva.
20%	(10 litres)	Delirium, swollen tongue and throat, deafness and dim vision, numb and shrivelled skin.

Thirst is, of course, the first sign of a need for water and this impulse should never be suppressed. In the desert, always drink when you feel like it, and when it's hot, keep drinking however you feel.

You can expect to take up to two weeks to acclimatise fully to the hot and dry desert environment. During this time you will tire easily, feel constantly hot, and perhaps experience a higher pulse rate than normal. Do not hesitate to drink as much as you need. Rationing your drinking habits in an attempt to be frugal is the last thing you should do. Instead, while on the piste, get used to using less water for other purposes, notably washing and cleaning, but also cooking. Soon, like everyone else, you will begin to appreciate water for the vital resource it is in the desert - never something to be squandered.

Acclimatisation is not just getting used to the heat. It is an actual physiological process whereby the sweat glands learn to secrete more water, thus enabling the body to maintain the crucial core temperature of 37°C through surface evaporation. Once acclimatised you will actually consume more water but, as long as you replenish what you have lost, you will feel comfortable.

Perspiration may not always be announced by soaking clothes and beads of sweat running down your temples. While riding, and in most conditions of heat and low humidity, sweat evaporates instantly and is one reason why you should keep exposed skin covered (sunburn being the other). Paradoxically, the hotter it gets, the more important it is to keep covered up and minimise water loss.

As a rule you should urinate as often as is normal, about four to five times a day. The colour of your urine should also remain the same as normal. A darker shade of yellow means that the toxins are becoming too concentrated in the solution, because you are not drinking enough or you are losing more through sweating. You must drink more under these circumstances.

In winter, and at higher altitudes, you might drink as little as a litre or so a day, excluding tea, etc. However, in summer your demand for water increases at an accelerated rate so that, at 38°C, just by sitting in the shade you are losing a litre per hour. Thus, in only five hours you will begin to feel seriously dehydrated. The body begins to lose increasing amounts of water as the average daily temperature begins to exceed 25°C. Agadez, in Niger, experiences these average temperatures for eleven months of the year.

Salt and the Human Body

When drinking large quantities of water, attention must also be paid to the loss of minerals dissolved in the sweat. The correct combination and concentration of salts is vital to the body's electrolytic balance. This governs the transmission of signals to the brain from the nervous system, and explains why your senses begin to malfunction as dehydration sets in. A slight deficiency of salt is characterised by headaches, lethargy and muscular cramps. Note that it may take a day or two for salt levels to be sufficiently depleted for these symptoms to become noticeable.

If you feel groggy, taking some salt in solution will make you feel better almost immediately, something that is likely to remind you to keep your salt intake on par with water consumption. In fact after any exertion, such as pushing your bike, mending a puncture or walking up dunes, a cup of salty water makes a refreshing drink and will instantly replenish the salt and water you have lost during your activity.

Salted water may not, however, be to everyone's taste. Licking some grains off the back of your hand, or taking salt tablets, both washed down with water, are alternatives. Too much salt in one go (an easy mistake to make with tablets) will make you nauseous and possibly induce vomiting, which takes you back to square one. Taking regular but moderate doses of salt is the simple way to prevent this mineral deficiency.

Water Purification

You should be sure that the water you drink is clean and does not contain any bacteria or other foreign bodies harmful to your well-being. Over three-quarters of the world's diseases - like typhoid, cholera, dysentery and bilharzia - are carried in water; all of them are endemic in Africa, although not necessarily in the Sahara.

Polluted water is most common around settlements and is caused by poor sanitary and hygienic practices contaminating possibly a single source of water. However, remote wells such as the one at Arbre du Ténéré and at Tlm Missao on the Tanezrouft can also become polluted. Both of these are vitally strategic sources of water in their areas. The Arbre well has long been marked as "*eau tres mauvaise*" on Michelin maps, since a dying animal fell into the well. The well at Tlm Missao is merely surrounded by dried-up carcasses of donkeys and goats, which may have been abandoned when a passing nomad encampment moved on. Although the water is clear and fresh, the clouds of flies thriving off the desiccated beasts make the sterilisation of water here advisable.

In Algeria, the water you get from taps is good enough to drink without any treatment, unless you have an especially sensitive stomach. In practice, while on the main pistes in Algeria, it is rare to depend entirely on water from wells, and tap water should always be used if available. Southern Tanezrouft wells tend to give rather opaque, sandy water which can be pre-filtered with a fine-weave Milbanks bag or a fine ceramic filter such as a Katadyn.

Methods of Purification

Water can be sterilised by filtering through microporous ceramic cores - a safe, non-chemical method - or through iodine or charcoal-impregnated elements. The pump-action filters which use the above methods (essential with a ceramic core) are much quicker than the gravity action filters.

Water can also be chemically sterilised with chlorine tablets or by using more effective silver or iodine (tablets or droplets) as sterilising agents. They are simply added to water but need to stand for a certain time, usually half an hour or so, until the chemicals take effect. Note that iodine can also be used as a disinfectant but it can be toxic in high doses.

These tablets are the easiest and most compact method of sterilising water, but they do not actually remove the impurities from the water. A cheap and easy way to do this is to use a filter bag of fine cloth which would remove most of the sediment and larger particles. These Milbanks bags can be washed and re-used but they're rarely actually necessary.

Some filters operate by inverting a small reservoir on to the filter, which allows the water to dribble through the core into your own vessel. They are extremely slow and are used more as back-ups for backpackers who would not be carrying the quantities of water needed for desert travel. Indeed, it might be possible to die of thirst waiting for some of these devices to produce drinkable water and their use is not recommended for the high volume demands of the desert biker.

Manually operated filter pumps, like the expensive but robust Swiss-made Katadyn, the similar Pur, or the smaller First Need are considerably quicker, producing about half a litre or more a minute, depending on the state of the water. Betina Selby used a Katadyn pocket filter fastidiously during her cycle ride along the river Nile to its source (*Riding the Desert Trail*). At times it meant repeated cleaning of its core while trying to extract drinkable water from the heavily silted waters of the Nile in Sudan, but her patience was rewarded by never getting sick.

The pump-operated filters are recommended for those travelling south of the Sahara, where warmer temperatures encourage greater bacteriological activity in the more humid conditions. Otherwise, tablets are adequate in most cases; the more expensive Micropur, from Katadyn are the most effective without affecting the water's taste.

Finally, if all else fails, you can always boil water for three minutes, which will kill most bacteria.

Water Filters

These aren't all the water filters available, just the ones recommended for desert biking use given the factors outlined above.

- **KATADYN** £215 (new core £132). Robust, microporous ceramic filter mechanically sterilises water and lasts for years with regular cleaning. Pumps up to 0.75 litres/min.

- **KATADYN MINI FILTER** £100 (new core £46). Uses the same method as above but at half the weight and price. Pumps 0.5 litres/min.

- **PUR EXPLORER** £149 (new core £70). A viable alternative to the established Katadyn, its self-cleaning facility resists clogging or fiddly cleaning while also featuring a sterilising iodine matrix. Pumps 1 litre/min.

- **PUR SCOUT** £90 (new core £32). Compact and simplified version of Explorer without self-cleaning option but retaining iodine matrix. Pumps 0.5 litres/ min. A carbon cartridge (£35) is available for both Pur models to remove excess chemicals, including residual iodine.

MSR WATERWORKS: £125 (new filter components £7, £22 and £30). Easily used pump with screen, membrane and carbon/ceramic filters progressively purifying and sterilising water. Can be fiddly to clean and maintain and not widely available. Pumps 0.7 litres/min.

- **FIRST NEED DELUXE:** £50 (new core £25). Microporous pump filter with core needing replacement after 400 litres but very good value for money. Pumps 0.5 litres/min.

- **PWP TREKKER TRAVEL WELL** £30. (new cartridge £15). Inexpensive and compact pump-filter with separate purifying and sterilising cartridges lasting up to 100 litres. Also a tinier Pocket Travel Well (£12): handy as emergency use. Pumps 0.2 litres/min.

- **MIL BANKS BAGS:** £15. Fine cloth pre-filter to removing excessive sediment and other particles from water. Use with above filters to extend their core lives or in conjunction with tablets listed below.

Water Purifying Chemicals

- **PURITABS** effective cost 4p/litre. Chlorine sterilising agent which leaves an unpleasant taste and smell.

- **MICROPUR** 9p/litre. Silver agent which leaves no taste or smell. Not toxic if overdosed and lasts for months.

- **POTABLE AQUA** 8p/litre. Iodine in a tablet form, can be toxic in overdose.

- **TINCTURE OF IODINE** 75p for 25 ml, 2-3 drops per litre. Can also be used as a disinfectant, but all iodine-based sterilising agents tend to lose their effectiveness after a while.

KEEPING HEALTHY

> Bentley (a journalist): *Tell me Major Lawrence, what is it that attracts you personally to the desert?*
> Lawrence, emphatically: *It's clean.*
>
> LAWRENCE OF ARABIA

THIS CHAPTER IS DELIBERATELY BRIEF and is intended only as a general introduction to the subject of travellers' health. Far greater knowledge about desert health care and survival can be found in Lascelles' excellent little book, *Stay Alive In The Desert* by Dr K.E.M. Melville (sadly, out of print). *The Travellers' Handbook* published by Wexas (£14.95) also has a good section on desert health and medicine as well as being exactly what its title says. If you're interested in your health then reading either *The Tropical Traveller* by John Hatt (£7.99) or *Travellers' Health* by Dr Richard Dawood (same price) will educate you or fill you with paranoia. As Peter O'Toole dryly observed in the film quoted above, the sterility of the desert does indeed make it a clean place, although this dryness can bring with it other problems and ailments.

First Aid Kit

A plastic lunch box is the ideal container for your First Aid kit, which should include the following:

- Aspirin or Paracetamol.

- Malaria pills (see below)

- Diocalm or Lomotil (prescription) for diarrhoea.

- Laxative for constipation (note that too much Lomotil can cause constipation).

- Thermometer.

- Antiseptic cream.

- Insect repellent.

- Multi-vitamins.

- Various dressings, plasters, bandages, gauze, safety pins, tape and cotton wool.

- Steristrips for closing wounds.

- Eye drops.

- Throat lozenges.

- Lip salve.

- Oil of cloves for toothaches.

- Ralgex spray or Deep Heat cream for aches and strains.

- A sterile syringe or two.

- A few sachets of Rehydrat or Dioryte powders for especially bad diarrhoea or heat exhaustion.

- If you are able to get some antibiotics and proper painkillers from a sympathetic GP, then so much the better.

Inoculations

For the Sahara, you will need the following inoculations, at the very least:

- Yellow Fever

- Tetanus

- Typhoid

- Polio

- Gamma Globulin

Protection against Hepatitis A is also useful but it doesn't protect you against the more virulent, but much less common, Hep' B from which one never really fully recovers. Hepatitis B is contracted in the same ways as AIDS i.e., through contact with infected saliva or blood. There is a new vaccine available for Hep B, however, which costs £25, about half the cost of all the above inoculations put together unless you are able to get them free, from your GP.

The cholera vaccine, absent from the recommended list, has proved to be barely effective and, in the words of Dr. Richard Dawood the million pounds spent annually on cholera vaccination in this country "is a complete waste of money". The World Health Organisation stopped publishing cholera vaccination certificates in 1989 and no longer recommends immunisation for travellers. An unofficial certificate's only value may be to facilitate entry at a remote border where the guard has not heard this latest news.

Acclimatisation

Travelling abroad, especially in Africa where nothing is predictable, puts you under a physical and mental stress which you may not immediately acknowledge. Acclimatising to the desert conditions can take up to a fortnight. During this time you can expect to feel lethargic, too hot or too cold, and become easily exhausted by physical activity. On your way south, as you learn to seek out shade whenever resting, your skin's sweat glands adapt to the increasing heat by secreting more sweat, so as to keep the core of your body at the correct temperature of 37°C. Therefore, as you acclimatise you will be drinking more water, rather than less. This thirst is quite normal and should not be suppressed. Sweating is the body's main thermoregulatory device and in hot climates sweating is always present, even if, due to the air's aridity, it evaporates instantly.

Unfortunately, the body has no way of controlling the loss of water in hot climates, and it must sweat to keep cool. The good thing is that the brain recognises this limitation and forces you to alter your behaviour by dressing in appropriate clothing and avoiding heavy manual labour, or any activity in the middle of the day. In short, keep cool and save energy by taking it easy for the first couple of weeks in hot weather, avoiding heat exhaustion. See the chapter on Water, for more information.

Nutrition

Probably more important than all the inoculations listed earlier is an attempt to maintain scrupulous cleanliness and hygiene, especially when it comes to water and eating the local food. In a restaurant this can be a bit of a gamble, but the appearance of the establishment ought to give a clue as to the quality of its food.

On a motorbike, your capacity for carrying substantial amounts of food for more than a few days is limited. Dried food, too, will depend on your supply of water, which is never really enough for all contingencies. Therefore, learning to cook what is locally available is a necessity and you should make the most of any fresh fruit and vegetables available.

In the Sahara, produce you will recognise includes onions, tomatoes, lettuce, potatoes, oranges, bananas and, of course, dates, as well as a variety of strange and exotic food that is just as good for you - provided it's all thoroughly washed in clean water. Most things may only be available in the larger towns and it is best to make the most of them as it is difficult to know when the next fresh food will be available. Don't be unduly wary of local food - it is quite safe as long as you are sensible and take the necessary precautions.

Ailments

In the desert, common ailments include:

• Colds and headaches

• Heat exhaustion

• Diarrhoea or constipation

• Dried and cracked lips, runny nose sore eyes and throat

• Burns and cuts to hands

• Sunburn

• Stress and fatigue

The first aid kit listed above will help you deal with most of these. Less common are some more serious ailments:

• **Heat Stroke** This is the result of serious dehydration. See the chapter on Water for how to remedy this situation.

• **Scorpion and Snake Bites** These are very rare and rarely fatal. The area around Ouargla in Algeria's oil fields is said to be especially infested with scorpions. Avoid rocky camp sites and shake out footwear in the mornings. Snakes are very shy but migrate towards sources of warmth at night.

• **Dysentery** A severe form of diarrhoea, it can be either amoebic or bacillary. Either is very debilitating, much more so than ordinary diarrhoea, and needs to be treated under skilled medical supervision, as blood or stool tests are required to diagnose the exact nature of the illness. Fluid levels must be maintained during these types of illness as extreme fluid loss can lead to dehydration and death. Dysentery is the main cause of Africa's appallingly high infant mortality.

• **Malaria** A good reason to stay in the desert is to avoid mosquitoes and the resultant risk of malaria, the most common cause of death in the world. Different drugs cover different areas and they are changing all the time as mosquitoes develop immunity to vaccines. If you ring the Malaria Reference Laboratory's Malaria Helpline, ☎01891 600350, they'll finally tell you (after a lot of other stuff) that for sub–Saharan Africa you'll need a Mefloquine (also known as Larium) tablet once a week and a Paludrine daily. Both these drugs are available from chemists without prescription and their courses should be followed to the letter. Travellers commonly contract malaria weeks or months after their journey is over because they did not complete the course. If you do get the disease, at best you will suffer from several days of debilitating fever. The best way to avoid getting malaria is to avoid getting bitten by mosquitoes: keep covered after dusk, use a repellent and mosquito net or tent, and avoid camp sites near stagnant water.

• **Rabies** Avoid petting cats and dogs or any other mammals, even if they are not foaming at the mouth. Excitable dogs are a common sight around villages and, as you may already know, dogs the world over go nuts at the sight of a helmeted rider. At all costs avoid being bitten by any beast in Africa. There is no reliable cure for rabies, which nearly always ends in delirium and death.

- **Bilharzia** This nasty disease is transmitted by a parasite that infests fresh water snails. It is endemic throughout Africa in all bodies of water other than fast-moving streams or at high altitude (for example, the gueltas - rock pools - in the desert mountains will be free of bilharzia, but not necessarily safe to drink or bathe in). Once you've read about the way bilharzia develops in a human organism, any desire you may have for refreshing yourself in a dubious water supply will be eradicated. If diagnosed early, however, bilharzia is easily curable.

- **Aids** (known as Slim in Africa) AIDS is now epidemic in Central and East Africa. Catching the HIV virus through heterosexual activity is much easier in the Third World due to the increased prevalence of internal, open sores borne by people who experience poor health care. If you expect to have sex with strangers, note that condoms are very rare in Africa, so bring your own. Condoms will also protect you from catching other venereal diseases and Hepatitis B. Being given a transfusion of infected blood, or being injected with infected needles is also a way of contracting Hep' B or the HIV virus. For this reason, you should include a syringe and a couple of unopened needles in your first aid kit.

Stress

One aspect of travel health that is rarely talked about is stress, usually what you come on holiday to get away from. It will come as no surprise that you're likely to find motorbiking around the Sahara, especially alone, just about the most stressful thing you've done in a long time. The obvious but often underestimated effects of 'culture shock' as well as fears of being robbed, murdered, getting lost or becoming ill are all the more acute when you're on your own with everything you possess for the next few weeks within arm's reach.

The need for constant vigilance can lead to the common symptoms of stress; headaches, irritability and, more commonly, absent-mindedness and susceptibility to minor ailments like colds. This kind of tension isn't made any easier by riding along remote desert tracks with only a little water and fuel for days at a time.

A common way to deal with these perceived threats is to keep moving to end your dangerous but heroic escapade as soon as possible. I have experienced this nervous restlessness in myself and others and have

recognised it for what it is; an inability to relax or trust anybody for fear that something bad is going to happen. This is different from the "running for your life" panic; when your long cherished adventure is falling to pieces about you, getting away from the seemingly menacing desert environment makes sense. It is not uncommon for overlanders who have taken long, hazardous but actually successful trans–continental journeys to have nightmares once they get back home, as the subconscious turns in on recent memories and ponders "what if that truck hadn't. . .", etc.

Fortunately, this understandable paranoia slowly abates, especially when you have had a chance to get used to your surroundings and meet local people (other than the authorities), who will offer you a generosity and hospitality that you rarely encounter elsewhere. Sadly, by the time you get to this level of psychological equilibrium you may be out of money and on your way home. I mention it here in the hope that you will not waste much of the trip for which you have planned for so long in useless paranoia - try and get as much out of the people you meet as out of the pistes you ride.

CLIMATE, LANDFORMS & WILDLIFE

CLIMATE

One might expect the inhabitants of the Sahara to get bored by their weather forecasts: another day of clear skies with high or very high temperatures, occasional sand storms and winds from the east or north east of 10-15 mph.

However, while the Saharan climate is extreme, with very high temperatures in the summer and little or no rain, it is also erratic. Average temperatures and rainfall, as they appear in the Michelin 953 map, are only a guide to the kind of weather you can expect in the Sahara at anytime. For example, Djanet may have an average daily maximum temperature in March of 26°C and less than 50mm of rainfall throughout the year. However, the month of March sees temperature rises of over a degree per week all over the Sahara, including Djanet. Also, any rain that might fall in Djanet is likely to be a single, spectacular downpour that would briefly flood the oued from torrents pouring off the Tassili's cliffs.

On a bike, exposed as you are to the elements, your visit to the desert must take into account the expected weather conditions as much as any other factors.

In northern Algeria annual temperatures are more varied than in the south where it remains either hot or very hot all the time. Ouargla, only 350 miles south of the Mediterranean, can be as cold as 4°C around New Year (average daily minimum) rising to 43°C in August (average daily maximum), probably more on some days. These are air temperatures in the shade and are about as hot as it gets anywhere in the Sahara; great weather for scorpions.

Most bike riders in Britain will be all too familiar with the sensation of riding in near-freezing temperatures, albeit at greater humidity. Properly wrapped up in all kinds of thermal gear so that you can hardly move, it can be a surprisingly tolerable experience as long as the Happy Eaters are not too far apart. Coming from this environment to ride in temperatures of over 40°C can be a real shock. Dehydration is relentless and extremely swift, sending a choking dryness creeping down your throat. You have to drink constantly, easily consuming up to ten litres of drinking water each day and through the night. The wind chill factor that makes winter riding in Britain so uncomfortable becomes the 'wind-wilt' factor in the Saharan hot season, when ambient temperatures rise above that of body heat (37°C) and oven-like wafts of 45°C heat will burn bare skin. At these kind of temperatures you actually have to wrap up against the extreme heat to limit the loss of your body fluids. By sealing your cuffs, collar and waist, a marginally moister sub-climate is created around your body which inhibits the rapid dehydration.

You have to experience this type of heat and dryness fully to appreciate the dramatic deterioration of the human body when dehydrated. Without water and shade, it's plain to see how survival would be impossible for more than a day or two in a Saharan summer. On a bike in mid-summer, even something as straightforward but laborious as mending a puncture in mid-afternoon scarcely bares thinking about.

Conversely, you may wake to find a fine frost covering your sleeping bag and the surrounding dunes. Frost is rare but freezing temperatures are common on most deep winter nights at high altitude. In the winter of 1991 there was a light fall of snow north of Ghardaia and one New Year's Eve and Tamanrasset was visited by a light drizzle that had no effect on the permanent water shortage that afflicts this town.

When to go

Visiting the deep Sahara during the summer months is out of the question unless you are very experienced and have some idea what to expect. A few years ago I recall reading in Motor Cycle News about a bunch of Honda Benly riders who thought they'd ride their 200cc commuter bikes to Tamanrasset for charity. Unfortunately they decided to turn their altruism into a stunt by riding in the middle of summer. At that time the tarmac surface deteriorated south of El Golea, a thousand kilometres from Tamanrasset. Sure enough this is where they and their hopelessly inappropriate machines turned back, beaten by the heat, the conditions and their own foolhardiness.

While a carefully planned summertime crossing may be accomplished with some discomfort, the extreme heat and dryness will demand water consumption of at least 6 litres per day. This accounts for drinking water only and will still leave you feeling tired, lethargic and susceptible to sickness.

Just by sitting still you are losing 2% of your body weight an hour at around 40°C. A sound bike will handle things much better than you, but the safety margins for motorbiking in the Sahara are narrow enough as they are and in summer the risk, especially for those new to the desert, is far too great.

October to March is the best time to visit the desert. The months of November and February are ideal, while in December and January it can get too cold for comfort north of Tamanrasset and the days are also annoyingly short.

Sandstorms and Duststorms

True desert sandstorms are a feature of the Sahelian summer and, less dramatically, the equivalent northern semi-arid zone south of the Atlas Mountains in the autumn. They are usually preceded by very hot, wind-less days when the advance of warm and humid air from ocean or sea into the hot, dry interior produces a huge wall of windborne sand thousands of metres high.

Riding into such a wall is like stepping out of an aeroplane in a storm. You are suddenly assaulted by high winds, stung by flying sand and pelt-ed with heavy rain drops, soon becoming completely disorientated. In the Sahel (the drought-stricken semi-arid zone bordering the southern Sahara) this is followed by a wonderful deluge of rain that transforms the desert for a day or two; the winds die down suddenly and the air becomes cool and fresh. In fact it's worth sticking out a Saharan summer just to witness this spectacular event.

Dust storms involve similarly disorientating high winds but without the following rain and they can occur at any time. In the heart of the desert these storms can last for days and can also involve very high lev-els of static electricity as the following account by Alisdair Kennedy records:

"Before sunset a wind got up from the northeast, unpleasantly hot and dry. The surface of the ground was lost in an ankle-deep carpet of moving sand and the trucks were pulled round to form a windbreak for the cooks. The air was heavy and oppressive. Out of the wind, the sweat began to pour off people, but once back in the wind it was sucked dry in an instant. Tempers grew short and people began to complain of headaches and feeling dizzy and unwell. Within a short time people were vomiting and "flaking out" with all the symptoms of heat exhaustion. A mix of salt and bicarb in water was made up, and even the most reluc-

tant were persuaded to drink at least half a pint before being sent off to wrap up against the wind which was dehydrating us all. As the wind increased the level of blowing sand rose higher and the tension seemed to grow in the air. Sparks leaped from the steel water tanks when the taps were opened, and small bolts of static jumped from the truck wheels to the frames of the camp beds in their lee.

At this time the duty group had been struggling bravely to cook a meal in the shelter of the trucks, but a sudden gust of wind scattered their screens and blew tables, stoves and all into the air. By sheer good luck, at that moment there had been no hot pans on the stove and the four cooks were able to extricate themselves from the wreckage unhurt. Camp beds took off and blew away into the darkness. Normally sane people stood swearing violently into the wind and blowing sand. A gritty meal was produced for those with stomach enough to eat it and the duty group had the thoroughly miserable task of washing up with water that rapidly became a sandy soup. Away from the turbulence caused by the trucks the blowing sand only reached knee height. Those who were not sleeping in the vehicles or on the roofs crawled into their sleeping bags out in the open, feet to the wind, heads and faces swathed in layers of cheche and towels, pinning down their camp beds as they climbed into them. As they wriggled down into the sweaty interiors, sudden lightening flashes of static began to play along the metal frames of the camp beds and then leap to the ground. From the yells and oaths, everyone in a nylon sleeping bag was having a suddenly painful experience. The bags were alive with static and to touch the frame of the bed gave a shock. Blue flashes crackled at the slightest movement and the sand sifted into bags, ears and noses. I saw one huddled shape lift its knees to get a bit of shelter and the sudden movement brought a sudden spate of static which lit up his bag from the inside!"

Riding on the tarmac during sand or dust storms is risky, especially on the fringes of the desert where there is more traffic. Continuing to ride on the piste is the most common way inexperienced get lost and disappear in the desert. Unless you are certain of the way ahead you must stop and sit it out. On a bike this might prove to be an uncomfortable couple of days, during which time your water reserves may be used up. However, such spectacular aeolionics are exceptional in the desert. Most often there is a light but constant breeze from the northeast during the day that settles down around dusk.

LANDFORMS IN THE SAHARA

Chances are that riding south down the highway from Algiers, your first impressions of the Sahara will be rather disappointing. Not until you are south of In Salah do you come across the first really big masses of dunes flanking the road, and only when you enter the Arak Gorge does the desert quickly lose its monotony. The gorge walls spread out into the ancient Mouydir Mountains, and you will have finally arrived in the varied and intriguing desert you have been expecting.

The Sahara sits on ancient crystalline rock as old as any on earth, formed over 2000 million years ago, in pre-Cambrian times. Like much of Africa, it is part of what geologists believe to have been the original continent known as Panagea. About 200 million years ago, when Panagea began breaking up under the tectonic forces of the churning magma, the five main continental masses which we see today were formed. That they appear to fit together so neatly supports the 'single original continent' theory.

Since that time, the original rock has been eroded, deposited and re–eroded by the actions of wind and water into fine, crystalline grains of silica known commonly as 'sand'.

Sand

Sand is the remains of igneous rock and the essence of some sedimentary rocks. Loose, in the form of dunes or compacted into layers of sandstone, it covers most of the surface of the Sahara. Despite the popular illusion, the great seas of dunes, known as *ergs* cover less than a sixth of the desert, but this is still half a million square miles, an area greater than Spain, France and Italy put together.

Despite the plausibility of windborne sand's erosive power (a sandstorm can render glass opaque) water is the chief weathering agent of Saharan rock. In more humid climatic epochs the bizarre canyons and towers of southeast Algeria's Tassili N'Ajjer were carved, the trachyte plugs of the Atakor Massif were exposed, while the resultant debris sifted down to form the great gravel plains which surround these exposed highland areas. It is these plains which make up most of the surface of the Sahara. The chief impression you get while riding down the trans–Saharan highway is cresting a ridge of hills to face an extensive and featureless plain out of which eventually looms another ridge of hills and an opportunity for a bit more bend swinging.

Spectacular view from Assekrem in the Hoggar Mountains
(M.Foster).

Mountains

In places, these sandy plains have been weathered away to expose the ancient granitic bedrock, such as at the Mouydir Mountains south of Arak or in the Hoggar. Alternatively the plains have been pierced by volcanic extrusions of lava to form distinctive basaltic peaks with columnar walls, as seen at Assekrem in the Hoggar. The highest peak in Chad's Tibesti Mountains, Emi Koussi, is an active volcano of over 10,000 feet in altitude, and the entire Tibesti is dotted with sulphurous springs of bubbling mud and volcanic cones. The less barren highlands of the Adrar Des Iforhas in northeastern Mali and the Aïr in Niger were similarly formed by the uplifting of the crust by volcanic extrusions, but greater weathering has denuded any distinctive volcanic formations.

Hammadas

Geologists have classified sedimentary plains of highland debris according to the extent of their weathering and erosion. The least eroded of these types of plains is known as a **hammada**, actually a plateau or high plain of rocks and stones of uniform size, interspersed with the occasional boulder, resistant to movement or degradation by wind or water. Here the bare rock has been broken down over millions of years by chemical and mechanical weathering. The bleak and barren Tademait plateau is a fairly advanced example of a hammada, covered in millions of sun-blackened

stones. Descending the escarpment on the way to In Salah you pass outlying remnants of the plateau's southern edge, resistant buttes surrounded by scree, similar in appearance to the plugs of the Atakor.

The rounded, wind-worn crags of Gara-Ekar, which you pass to the
west on the way to In Guezzam on Algeria's southern frontier, are
regarded as the remains of a completely worn down hammada appearing as sandstone monoliths surrounded by sand.

Regs and Serir

Once a hammada has passed a certain point of denudation it becomes a
reg. These plains bear the water-borne detritus of past plateaux and
present mountain ranges, fed by long–vanished rivers. The finer sediment of smaller sized stones, pebbles or gravel is carried further from
its source, eventually becoming **serir**; a plain of fine sand that has been
washed or blown far away from its place of origin. Thus the northern
Ténéré is classified as reg, a coarser grained plain of gravel close to the
Aïr and Hoggar highlands, while further south the Ténéré becomes serir,
a glaring, featureless sand plain.

Ergs and Barchan Dunes

And beyond the serir are the big sand seas or **ergs**. In the Ténéré the
Grand Erg de Bilma is just part of a massive area of dunes stretching
from the Aïr to western Chad. Dunes are the most common land form
associated with the desert and indeed these extraordinarily beautiful
features are a highlight of anyone's visit. Just how the wind is able to
form the precise curves, slopes and margins of ergs has yet to be fully
understood. Why doesn't an erg become serir under the action of wind
and gravity? That something so graceful and exquisite could theoretical-
ly be blown away in the first sandstorm is part of the beauty and mystery of the dunes.

Away from the chaotic jumble of the impenetrable ergs is found the
classic sand dune known as a barchan, an elongated crescent shape with
its 'horns' pointing down wind. The windward side is often firm enough
to ride over with reduced tyre pressures, but as you near the slip face
the sand becomes much softer so that it's barely possible to crawl up a
dune's slip face.

Barchan dunes are regarded as mounds of sand that have been fairly logically shaped by the prevailing wind. But again, why one should find

a barchan in the middle of a desolate reg is anyone's guess. One early theory suggested that a dead beast or old tyre creates its own turbulence in the prevailing wind, initiating deposition and accumulation of sand, which eventually gives rise to a solitary dune. However, since digging up (digging down?) a few barchans doesn't reveal a camel's skull or other discarded items, this theory doesn't stand up. It's possible that once they reach a certain size barchans become mobile, leaving behind the item which created them, but science just hasn't found all the answers yet.

Oueds

More familiarly known as wadis, oueds are the courses of dried river beds or creeks and vary from a barely distinguishable line of fine sand to a towering, wooded canyon carved through the rocks. Larger oueds can be useful aids to navigation; many routes in the Sahara follow the courses of oueds to assist with orientation. Oueds also provide habitats for numerous forms of wildlife and vegetation, such as along the Oued Tilemsi in Mali. Extraordinarily, it is said that more people have drowned in the Sahara in flash floods then have died of thirst. For this reason you should not camp in oueds during unsettled weather, despite the comfort and shelter they can afford compared to the open plain.

Fossils

That the whole of the Sahara was once a sea bed is evident from the fossils displayed in recently exposed cliffs. Prehistoric fish, ammonites and other long extinct crustaceans are easily found, for example, along the Tinterhert escarpment south of the Ohanet road in eastern Algeria

West of the Tinterhert, along the Mirabel piste that slips under the southern edge of the Grand Erg Oriental, giant trees from the dinosaur era (about 120 million years ago) have been petrified into slate-black rock. The crumbled sections of trunk, up to four feet in diameter, lie alongside the piste while the surrounding desert floor is littered with broken fragments of fossilised wood. Evidence of petrified forests can also be seen to the west of In Salah on the Aoulef piste, and near In Gall, west of Agadez in Niger.

In parts of the Ténéré the sand is composed of crumbled sea shells, something you'll also find along the Dhar Tlchit piste in Mauritania, although here at least, the shells may be remnants of Neolithic jewellery or even Stone Age currency. Elsewhere, a dinosaur cemetery has been found in the dunes of Gadoufaoua in the western Ténéré. The site is closely guarded as it's said to include an entire intact fossilised skeleton of a dinosaur lying in the sand - something which palaeontologists very rarely find. It was the subject of a British Natural History Museum expedition in 1989, and though cut short by political tremors in Niger, the expedition was delighted to find complete rows of gigantic backbones with individual vertebrae the size of basketballs. A cast of a dinosaur's skeleton from Gadoufaoua as well as many other interesting ethno-historical artefacts can be found in Niamey's excellent Musée National.

Collectors of geological oddities will be pleased to know that just south of El Golea they can encounter children standing fearlessly in the road, gesticulating desperately in an attempt to sell you a sand rose, another of the desert's incomprehensibly exquisite marvels of nature which 'grow' nearby. Sand roses are the result of evaporation of moisture and the subsequent crystallisation of sand with a heavy gypsum mineral content. The planes of interwoven 'petals' give the orangey-pink formation its rose-like appearance.

CAMELS AND OTHER WILDLIFE

The one form of wildlife everyone associates with the Sahara, the camel – 'ship of the desert' and, in Koranic lore, sole retainer of the hundredth name of Allah – is, paradoxically, not wild at all. Introduced into North Africa from the Middle East during Roman times, when increasing desertification was reducing the effectiveness of horses and donkeys, today's camels are all domesticated beasts which belong to someone, somewhere.

Indeed these roaming herds, which wander wherever pasture endures, are traditionally the basis of a nomad's wealth. A nomad without a camel in the Sahara would be as helpless as you without your bike. The pride and care a nomad bestows on his sometimes comical, cantankerous and, to us, ugly beast is a measure of the esteem with which they regard this intelligent and supremely adapted creature.

A camel may be able to go without water for weeks, but it needs to eat a little daily – roughly the opposite of human needs. Thus, the camel caravans or *azalai* which cross the Ténéré from Agadez to Bilma must carry giant bundles of fodder to sustain them during the weeks it will take to return to the sparse pasture of the Aïr foothills near Agadez. As well as food, the azalai carries goods which it will trade for salt and dates at Fachi and Bilma. It's 400 miles to Bilma from Agadez and by marching relentlessly, for up to twelve hours a day, the journey will take, "*ainsh*

Allah", about three weeks. During this time the camels will have survived on the water stored in their body tissues and not, as is commonly thought, in the hump. This instead stores most of the camel's fat and can provide nutrition for up to half a year at a time if not denuded by hauling burdens across the desert.

The camel may be adept at storing water, but its real skill is in not losing it in the first place, achieved by a variety of physiological feats. While we shrivel up into bits of toast just by sitting under a palm tree on a very hot day, a camel is able to endure body temperatures 10°C above normal. Only the brain needs to remain at the normal temperature and this is achieved with a profusion of blood vessels keeping this area at a crucial 37°C. Moreover, the camel is also able to control the viscosity of the blood in its circulatory system, which prevents the heart from struggling to pump thickening blood to the muscles. In humans, it is this sudden thickening of blood during the final stages of dehydration which causes the fatal escalation of temperature and eventual coronary seizure. When needs must, a camel can also reduce the rate of water filtered through its kidneys and subsequently lost through urination. Weight for weight, a human being loses water a hundred times faster than a camel in the same conditions. These are but a few of the tricks a camel has evolved to survive so capably in the desert.

Despite all these water retaining devices a camel will still lose up to a third of its body weight (around 160kg in a mature bull) over a period of weeks, though it can then regain it in a matter of minutes by drinking as much as 160 litres of water with no ill effects. However, this kind of water loss is extreme and by being pushed hard a camel is unlikely to achieve an ordinary life span of about 40 years.

A hardworking camel may not look under any particular duress (they barely sweat) lugging a quarter of a ton of salt up a dune, but when it finally drops to the ground in exhaustion, death is not far away. When this occurs or it suffers a debilitating injury to the legs, its owner will turn the dying beast's head towards Mecca and, with a brief prayer, cut its throat. He will then butcher it for an unexpected stew that evening and sell the remains of the meat. All desert nomads have this unsentimental, fatalistic but rarely cruel relationship with their camels.

And yet, like us, camels are sensitive to changes in their environment. A beast bred in the mountains may well suffer a brief, agoraphobic panic as it is led out into a Ténéré–like wilderness. Similarly, a plains camel, with its wide, flat feet so suited to flotation in soft sand, would need 'socks', as Wilfred Thesiger's Bedu companions provided at times, for walking over rocky terrain, which would otherwise ruin their soft foot pads.

Other Mammals

Because of their ability to endure the daytime heat, camels are by far the most conspicuous large mammals in the desert. However, other hoofed mammals such as the Addax, Oryx and Dorcas Gazelle have adopted similar devices as the savannah of only a few thousand years ago turned to desert. Amazingly, these varieties of antelope need never drink at all, extracting what water they need from the tufts of grass for which they spend their entire lives foraging for in the dunes of the southern Ténéré. These days, the Addax and Oryx are rarely seen, having been decimated by hunting and persistent droughts. The smaller, lithe dorcas gazelle is more common, surviving in isolation along the Dhar Tichit escarpment in Mauritania and the Oued Tilemsi in Mali, despite a concerted slaughter by hunters equipped with machine guns in the 1970's.

The shaggy mountain goat, or mouflon, is rarer still. An inhabitant of inaccessible rocky highlands, such as the Tassili N'Ajjer in southeast Algeria, they were the object of a quest by Jeremy Swift in his excellent study of the Saharan environment (see Books). After following a mouflon's spoor and tracks for days he was eventually rewarded with a blurred, telephoto shot of a startled mouflon running for cover. Another mammal that you will be lucky to see is the giant-eared fennec (see p.14 of the Sahara Handbook for a great picture!) a fox-like creature (but not a desert fox) that has become a victim of its own cuteness to European pet collectors. You may be less curious to encounter hyenas and jackals, which make a living scavenging around settlements but have even been known to attack and drag away grown adults in their search for nourishment.

One tiny mammal you will certainly spot, as you prepare your evening meal in a sandy area, is the gerbil and its cousins, the jerboa and sand rat. With their large, dark eyes, which enable nocturnal hunting for insects, these curious and yet incredibly jumpy rodents (in German known as "spring mouse") will gnaw through anything behind your back, only to scatter frantically as you turn. These are harmless enough, but can cause you a severe panic as they scratch around in the middle of the night. As you jump out of your skin at the thought of a giant tarantula or carnivorous lizard, the culprit turns out to be nothing more than a little hunched up gerbil panting guiltily from a nearby nook.

Reptiles and Insects

Reptiles and insects are the most prolific forms of life in the desert, but are almost inconspicuous to the passing motorised traveller. Only when you slow down to a more natural pace might you notice them – though even then most desert reptiles and insects are active only under cover of darkness as the numerous tracks across the morning sand will testify.

Lizards – such as iguanas, sand fish, geckos and monitors – are all victims of their dependency on the warmth of the sun. In the morning they must bask until they have warmed up enough to function properly. In this moment of vulnerability they could make a fitting breakfast for a passing fennec. And if they survive their daily warm-up they must then find shelter from the heat, as the sun passes its zenith, by burrowing under the sand or hiding in a rocky crevice until the evening brings the desert to life again. Like all desert fauna, lizards' and insects' paramount considerations are the acquisition and retention of water. This is done by avoiding daytime activity and aided by their skin or shells which limit the transpiration of body fluids. This in turn makes them the sole source of water for their predators.

Despite their fearsome appearance, none of the spiders common in the south Sahara – tarantulas, wind scorpions or camel spiders - will do more than deliver you a slight, venomless nip and the fright of your life. However, see the box below for details of the Horned Viper and some lethal scorpions.

Birds

The White Rumped Black Chat is an inquisitive bird seen in the northern desert, while the similarly plumed mourning wheatear darts around the Ténéré and southern Sahara. Other birds indigenous to the desert include sand grouse of spotted and chestnut-bellied varieties, which carry water to their chicks within their downy breast feathers. In the rocky plateaux, beady eyed ravens hop from rock to rock, while in the Aïr Mountains, one of the best sites in the Sahara for wildlife, you can still find the occasional ostrich (as well as some of the aforementioned antelopes.

As you can tell, Saharan avians aren't my forte; for a considerably more detailed account of Saharan bird life read the excellent *Field Guide to the Birds of West Africa* (£14.99) by W. Serle, G.J. Moral and W. Hartwig. It includes the indigenous birds as well as the migratory species which pass over the Sahara in their thousands in winter. Collins also produce other field guides to the animals of Africa. Hachette's *Guide du*

Sahara (see Books) has a good illustrated section on Saharan fauna segregated into their typical environments of ergs, oueds, rocky areas and so on.

DESERT DOCUMENTS

THE DOCUMENTATION AND BUREAUCRACY is one thing that puts many people off from travelling abroad. The documents listed below will be sufficient to get you to most ends of the earth, but may, have to be supplemented with additional local paperwork. For this reason it is worth buying yourself a king-sized wallet before you leave.

Passports and Visas

None of the North African countries will be pleased to see an Israeli stamp in your passport. In Niger and Mali, the police roadblocks love to fill your passport with "*vu en passage*" stamps at regular roadblocks, and possibly charge you for this service. Be sure that your passport has enough room to accommodate these stamps and any subsequent visas you may need on the way. Visas usually take up a whole page. Carry additional passport photos for visa applications en route as well as other permits. They can also make a customary gift to friends you make on the way.

Vehicle Registration Document

Your VRD (known as "*carte gris*" in French) is an essential requirement. Each country's border officials will be keen to see it and to check the details of engine and frame numbers, especially when leaving Algeria from the south. Be certain that all the numbers on your bike are clear and match your VRD.

International Driving Permit

You can get an IDP from any AA or RAC office – you don't have to join and it's issued on the spot. You need to show your license and supply a passport photo plus around £3.50. Don't expect much up-to-date information from either organisation about motorbiking in Africa, even if you're a member.

Carnet de Passages en Douane and *Laissez Passer*

The motoring organisations will undoubtedly tell you that you need a *Carnet de Passages en Douane*, or carnet for short. This important document guarantees that the country you are visiting will be paid all relevant duties should you sell your machine or somehow leave without it. Unfortunately, this makes abandoning your bike or having it genuinely stolen, a rather complicated business. Getting a carnet requires that you leave the RAC/AA's estimated value of your machine in a closed bank account, with the amount not released until the correctly stamped document is returned to them on your return. Banks will also stand surety if they believe you have sufficient assets. An insurance alternative exists to putting up the value of your machine - for poor riders of expensive machines, this is the best solution (see under Campbell Irvine, in Useful Addresses).

For the countries of the central and western Sahara, with which this book is mainly concerned, a carnet is not necessary, although it almost certainly will be for a longer, trans–African trip. Even in Mauritania, a ferry ticket back to Marseille was enough to convince the bemused customs of officers that we did not intend to leave without our vehicles. Niger and Mali have their own forms, called *Laissez Passer*, which you buy at the border and renew as necessary.

Vehicle Insurance

Green Card insurance can be used in Morocco and Tunisia. Everywhere else you must buy your motor insurance at the border. In Algeria insurance works out at about a pound a day, or less. See under Algeria, in Country Details for the complex entry formalities.

Travel Insurance

Motorbiking in the Sahara could justly be included under the 'hazardous' exclusion clauses of most travel and medical insurance policies. However, Campbell Irvine (see Useful Addresses) are experienced in supplying short-term travel insurance for overland expeditions. Ask for their blue form but remember that insurance is only a piece of paper until you can get to a phone box and let people know you're in trouble.

Money

Cash, in the form of French Francs, is the best type of currency to carry in the countries of the Sahara and West Africa. In Algeria, you must declare all your valuables on entry and exchange the equivalent of 1000 dinars. As in Mauritania, you must fill in currency declaration forms, which may be checked on departure. Keep any receipts for any further official currency transactions you make during your stay. In Algeria only, currency or valuables that you omit to declare can be exchanged easily on the black market. Depending on where you are, expect to get between three to six times the official rate of exchange. Every merchant, trucker or businessman you meet will find you before you find them, but keep your wits about you. Dealing like this is strictly illegal, and to get set-up and caught does not bear thinking about. If you feel uncomfortable or harassed by an illegal transaction, walk away.

The inoculations you will require before leaving for West Africa include yellow fever, cholera, tetanus, typhoid, polio and gamma globulin. For more details, see chapter on Health. None of these inoculations will guarantee that you won't get sick, but some border controls, notably in Niger, will not allow you to enter without a valid inoculation certificate for Yellow Fever. People have had to drive back to Tamanrasset from Assamaka, a distance of 400km, because they didn't have a Yellow Fever certificate.

MAPS

The following list does not include all the maps available for the Sahara, but instead recommends a selection of sheets to the most likely visited areas.

Stanfords Map Shop is the first place to start looking for special maps. They'll send you a catalogue detailing their North and West Africa coverage, which is very comprehensive, but bear in mind that IGN l:lm sheets (see below) are available from Paris for about half Stanfords' price. If you are buying several, get them by mail or in person from Paris. See Useful Addresses for Stanfords' and IGN's addresses.

• MICHELIN 953, North & West Africa. 1:4million (about £4). The best small-scale route-planning map for the majority of the Sahara. Sheet 954 covers North East Africa and Arabia; 955 covers Southern Africa There is also a Michelin 969 map that covers Morocco at various scales. The Hallwag l:lm map of Morocco also gives good, up to date detail of the remote areas south of the Atlas.

• INSTITUT GEOGRAPHIQUE NATIONAL, or IGN. Their l:lm sheets cover all of what was once French West Africa. Although some sheets are nearly 30 years old, they are still remarkably detailed and are an essential navigational aid if you are travelling off the main Saharan pistes. Similarly detailed 1:500,000 and 1:200,000 sheets (where lcm = 2km) are available from the Paris shop, although Stanfords carry some l:200,000s. At this scale the map shows every oued, outcrop and hill, but the black-and-white photocopies at Stanfords can be rather hard to follow. All IGN maps are originally in colour. Note that for sheets in scales greater than l:lm covering Niger and Mali, authority must be sought from that country before IGN can supply them.

IGN have also produced an updated series of "*pays et villes du monde*" maps which include many former French West African countries such as Senegal, Mali, Mauritania, Chad. Produced at scales between 1:1 and 1:2 million, the series, designated '3615', is more user friendly than the 'proper' IGN sheets but is expensive at nearly £8 a map

• The U.S. DEFENSE MAPPING AGENCY has been busy flying over the Sahara, producing Operational Navigation Charts (ONC) at 1:1 mil}ion, and Tactical Pilotage Charts (TPC) at 1:500,000 scale. These satellite produced pilots' charts are great on maximum elevations, airfield installations and topography, but skip all other terrestrial details like old forts, villages and useful landmarks. Like the black-and-white IGNs, they show every piste and obsolete camel track with no differentiation, and so have to be studied carefully to discern the main piste from the mass of tracks shown. Despite this limitation, the TPC H3D 1:500,000 sheet, while not being the sort of thing you can open out in a sandstorm, covers the interesting and popular area of the Tassili N'Ajjer in southeast Algeria, from In Amenas to Djanet and west to the Hoggar foothills. It is big enough to mark on the main pistes, major landmarks and other corrections without looking messy. ONCs, covering a greater area at 1:1m are less useful. Both are available from Stanfords for £8 each.

WEST MEDITERRANEAN FERRIES

THERE ARE twelve direct ferry routes from the European mainland to Morocco, Algeria and Tunisia, although **at present all services to Algeria are suspended due to the threat of terrorism**. Call SNCM in London (see Useful Addresses) to see what the latest situation is with the Algerian routes or go via Morocco or Tunisia. Which one you choose basically depends on whether you want to spend less time on European roads and more at sea, or vice versa. Your destination in the Sahara will also have a bearing on your ferry route, though none of the North African ports are more than a couple of days' ride away from the desert. The *ABC World Shipping Guide* (revised monthly) is a useful guide available from reference libraries and travel agents.

Shipping Back

The Shipping Guide will also detail services to and from European ports to places such as Dakar, if this is what you have in mind. Shipping your bike back can save time although the agreeable idea of travelling on board with your bike (if possible) back to Europe will probably cost you about twice the equivalent air fare. When you leave your bike in the docks expect any pilferable items to go missing during the voyage. Try and avoid giving them the keys (a bike can be pushed on board) and if you must do so, keep a spare set. Sharing a container with a vehicle is much more secure and, if you can come to an arrangement, probably cheaper. Don't forget to get your carnet stamped from the port authority, if necessary.

CROSSING FROM SPAIN

The shortest ferry crossings (taking less than an hour) are across the Straits of Gibraltar: from Algeciras in Spain to Tangiers or to the Spanish enclave of Ceuta in Morocco. This route now runs a hydrofoil service which is even quicker and is also a much cheaper option

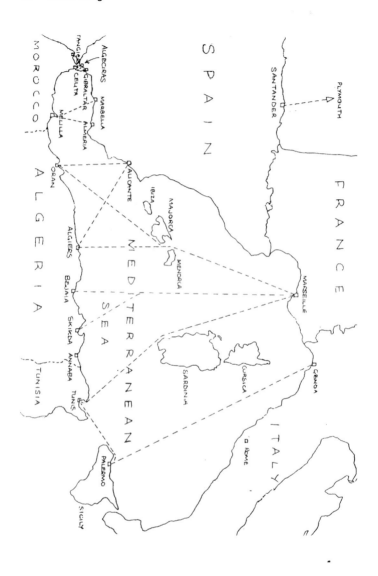

Ferry Routes to West Africa

than the Tangiers run. Ferries to Morocco run several times a day, all year round, and so making reservations in advance is not necessary - there is always room for a bike.

Other ferries across the Mediterranean are more frequent at peak holiday times and much less so in mid-winter, which is when you may be timing your visit, so bear this in mind when planning your trip.

The other Spanish enclave in Morocco, Melilla, is served three times a week from Malaga or Almeria in southern Spain, the journey taking seven hours. There is also a weekly service from Alicante to Oran in Algeria. However this service costs the same as all the other SNCM (Societe National Maritime Corse-Mediterranée) routes, so unless you happen to be near Alicante, you will have far more choice of times and destinations if you travel from MarseillE.

CROSSING FROM FRANCE

Marseille is southern Europe's busiest passenger port for ferries across the western Mediterranean to North Africa. From here ferries operate every other day to Oran or Algiers, taking as little as 20 hours (to Algiers).

Far less frequent are similarly priced ferries to Bejaia, Skikda and Annaba on Algeria's eastern seaboard, though it may not be a bad idea to arrive at one of these smaller ports in preference to the chaotic and intimidating main port/cities.

The Marseille to Tunis route costs about 15% less than the Algiers fare, and consequently is by far the cheapest way to arrive in North Africa for the least road miles from Britain. Also, because Tunisia is a preferred North African destination for European tourists, SNCM save their more modern and comfortable ships for this route. It would be worth timing your crossing to coincide with the gleaming white *Liberté Esterel* and *Napoleon* ferries, which offer cleanliness, showers and sit-down toilets, comfort, stability and reliability. They don't operate on every run to Tunis, so check your timetables and note that they are an adequate replacement for the long suspended DFDS service from Genoa, which the Glens rave about in the Sahara Handbook. Therefore, unless you like it rough (and there will be plenty of time for that later) avoid SNCM crossings on the "infamous four" ferries: the *Zeralda*, *El Djazair*, *Tipasa* and *Hoggar*.

All crossings from Marseille take a day and a night, and food is expensive so you may wish to stock up with French goodies and bottled water before you depart.

Tickets

Open return tickets are valid for up to a year, and you can claim a full refund before that time, in case your plans or itinerary change. Buying a return ticket in Algeria is complicated and expensive, not least because the ticket must be paid for in hard currency and not in the Algerian dinars which you may have acquired at a bargain rate (see Desert Documents) during your stay.

Southern Ferries, the British agent for SNCM can supply you with lists of sailings back to Marseille from your preferred port (including the all-important ship's name). Note that embarkation takes several hours and the ships rarely leave on time. Mechanical delays are common on the "infamous four". A friend once spent three days on the Hoggar during the Mediterranean storms in February 1989.

Outward journeys, especially around Christmas when many Algerians working in France go home for the holidays, should be booked a few weeks in advance. The preposterously overloaded cars of the 'guestworkers' are often thoroughly searched on arrival in Algiers, but tourists, and especially bikers, are rarely troubled. However, the officials are not beyond sending you back if some aspect of your documentation is not in order.

Bikes are classified as anything over 100cc; less than a 100cc is classified as baggage. Your gear is probably safer in the hold than it is on deck. You certainly shouldn't leave anything you are not prepared to lose in the four-berth cabins (offered at a small supplement), which are lockable only from the inside and are often visited by foot passengers looking for a vacant bunk.

Crossing from Italy

There are also ferries from Genoa to Palermo in Sicily, where ferries leave from Palermo and Trapani for Tunis, but this is an expensive option unless you are visiting Italy on your way out.

FERRY FACTS

Prices given are-one way, passenger–only fares. On all these routes the cost of a bike is about 50% of the passenger fare, though SNCM offer various discounts which can substatially reduce the cost. For latest details on all routes consult the *ABC World Shipping Guide*. Nothing is ailing to Algeria at the present time (July 1995).

ROUTE	FREQUENCY	COST (approx)	DURATION
Algeciras - Tangier	Every couple of hours	£14	1 hour
Algeciras - Ceuta	Several a da	£14	30 minutes
Malaga - Melillia	per week	£30	8 hours

Almeria - Melillia	3 per week	£33	7 hours
Alicante - Oran	2-5 per week	£175	12 hours
Alicante - Algiers	2-3 per week	£175	14 hours
Marseille - Oran	Every 3-6 days	£175	32 hours
Marseille - Algiers	Every 2-3 days	£160	20 hours
Marseille - Bejaia	1-3 a month	£160	24 hours
Marseille - Skikda	1-3 a month	£160	24 hours
Marseille – Annaba	1 or 2 a month	£160	24 hours
Marseille - Tunis	4-5 per month	£115	26 hours
Genoa - Palermo	2-3 per week	£88	23 hours
Scicily - Tunis	A few a week	£76	4 hours

COUNTRY DETAILS

WHAT FOLLOWS PROVIDES a general overview of the Saharan countries, with a brief description of the off-road riding opportunities there. If you're looking for more detailed information the appropriate books from Rough Guides or Lonely Planet are recommended as practical guides for the independent traveller.

ALGERIA

Unfortunately, at the time of writing, the political unrest which has troubled Algeria since the early 1990s shows no sign of abating, despite occasionally quiet periods. Foreigners have been targets of violence and a visit, certainly to the populous north is not recommended. If you insist on going and are able to get a visa, enter the country through southern Tunisia or southeastern Morocco and keep a very low profile. Avoid towns for any longer than necessary. Situations as reported overseas are often worse than they actually are, but at present a visit to Algeria will mean putting your property and your life in jeopardy.

Details given below predate the troubles.

- **Capital** Algiers.

- **Population** 25 million, mostly Berber, Arab and in the south, Tuareg.

- **Languages** Arabic, French and Tamachek.

- **Visas** Required by British nationals.

- **Consulates in Algiers** The British consulate is at 7 Chemin de Ayones but is presently unoccupied. There is a Malian consulate in Tamanrasset.

- **Border Formalities** As with all frontiers in Africa, have all your documents, a pen and if you smoke, a full packet to hand. At the port of Algiers this is the sequence:

    ◊ *Jump the queue because you're on a bike.*

    ◊ *Latch on to someone who reads French, if you don't.*

    ◊ *Fill in the green and white cards which are lying around somewhere near the entrance to the customs hall.*

    ◊ *Get your passport stamped by immigration, handing over both of the cards.*

◊ *Get your stamp checked and possibly be searched by customs.*

◊ *Fill in currency declaration form in duplicate.*

◊ *Fill in carte touristique. Under 'accommodation during your stay?', writing "Camping Ghardaia, Tamanrasset" used to be sufficient. This document is also a laissez passer for your bike. A carnet is not necessary in Algeria.*

◊ *Change at least 1000 dinars (see below) at the bank booth while making sure they stamp your forms and give you a receipt for the transaction.*

◊ *Proceed to SAA booth (the national insurance company) and buy insurance for the duration of your anticipated stay. It can be extended down south, but is much cheaper to buy at the docks.*

◊ *Finally, before you leave the docks your documents will be checked once again to see if they are all in order.*

The above procedure takes at least a couple of hours and has been, explained in full to prevent too much 'returning to Go' in what may be your first taste of full-blooded African bureaucracy. Algerian border officials are courteous and uncorrupt.

• **Currency** Dinar (DA). In April 1994 40 dinars equalled £1. You must change the equivalent of 1000 DA (around £25) before you leave the country, best done at the port of entry.

• **Accommodation** The main towns in Algeria have proper hotels, which are very expensive at the official rate of exchange. There used to be a very attractive campsite in Ghardaia (Camping M'zab, with hot showers) and increasingly spartan sites at Tamanrassret (busy), Djanet (expensive), In Salah (a dump) and Arak (epic location). These are all commonly used by tourists and are good places to meet up with other travellers, if you wish. Otherwise, the desert, away from prying eyes, is all yours and free.

• **Costs** At the official rate, Algeria is expensive to visit. However, petrol is about two-thirds of the UK price and diesel is virtually free. A diesel Land Rover can cover the same distance as a bike in Algeria for a third of the cost, but by sleeping out and using your wits (see Desert Documents), Algeria and its desert can be a bargain.

• **Desert Pistes** Algeria, the second biggest country in Africa (and tenth biggest h the world) is the best place to wear out your Michelin Deserts. There are many clearly defined pistes that are within the range of a well-prepared bike. Without the expense and risk of actually 'crossing the Sahara', you can get right into the heart of the desert. An ideal first-timer's route (which is by no means straightforward) is the 3600 kilometre loop from Ghardaia to Illizi, Djanet, Tamanrasset and back north again. About a third of this is off-road.

CHAD

While the difficult route from Nguigumi (Niger) around the shrivelling Lake Chad to the capital, N'djamena, remains open for the stubborn and patient (see Bradt's *Through Africa* for a taste of what to expect), that's about it as far as Chad goes. Even leaving the capital requires permit after permit. The track to Abeche and thence Sudan may be permissible, although the north, including the volcanic Tibesti Mountains, is beginning to open up very slowly, but only to well planned expeditions, it seems. The German adventure bike tour company *Wüstenfahrer* (see Usefu Addresses), is hoping to visit this area in March 1996. This area has been closed since the 1970's following a civil war supported openly by the Libyans and covertly by the French Foreign Legion. John Julius Norwich's Sahara (see Books) is an excellent account of a drive to the Tibesti and back from Djanet, and brims with Saharan wisdom.

LIBYA

Although contemporary politics are of little interest to the people who live in the desert, you should still think carefully before considering visiting Libya. Certainly safer than Algeria at the moment, independent tourists are beginning to focus on this country which has been little visited since the Islamic Revolution. Nevertheless, in the desert tourists are still a very rare sight and susceptible to good old fashioned banditry. Note that French is unknown and English rarely spoken. If you want to communicate you'll have to learn some elementary Arabic.

A Libyan visa can be obtained in the UK for £20 but would not guarantee entry into the country. The best place to try would be from southern Tunisia. For the latest information on Libya check out the latest edition of the *North African Handbook* (Trade & Travel; £14.95) or Lonely Planet's *North Africa on a Shoestring* (£15.95).

MALI

- **Capital** Bamako.

- **Population** 8 million. A mixture of Malinke, Bambara, Dogon, Songhai, Fula and Moors, all spread out regionally with Tuareg in the northeast.

- **Languages** French is the most widely spoken and understood, otherwise take your pick from the many indigenous tongues.

- **Visas** Required by all except French and West Africans.

- **Consulates in Bamako include;** Algeria, Mauritania, Senegal, Guinea, France and USA.

Fueling up in Nara (Mali) on the way to Nema in Mauritania.

- **Border Formalities** Not as bad as they used to be, but still slow and prone to a little mischievous corruption. Be prepared to have to give something - not necessarily money - and be flexible and patient. Buy a laissez passer or show carnet and insurance (see Niger, below). Show cholera (but see Keeping Healthy) and yellow fever certificates. Roadside police checks stamp your passport regularly east and north of Mopti.

- **Currency** CFA (Communaute Financière Africaine), tied permanently to the French Franc at 100 CFA for 1 FF. You can order CFA from British banks but specify CFA west otherwise you will probably be given CFA east (usually from Chad or Gabon). The latter are a bit like Scottish fivers in England and are best exchanged in a local bank for CFA west, as they can cause puzzled scrutiny or even refusal in remote areas. If you are really stuck you can pay in French Francs, which most people recognise and don't mind accepting in lieu of CFA. The countries of the CFA west zone are: Senegal; Mali; Burkina Faso; Ivory Coast; Togo; Benin and Niger.

- **Accommodation** Campements, rural resthouse/campsites with huts and sometimes a canteen, are the best bet for cheap accommodation. Otherwise you are best off sleeping out which, in the Sahel and southern woodlands, can mean mosquitoes and larger beasties. Hotels do exist: most are charming, rough and expensive but Mali is the sort of place where unexpected offers of accommodation (and anything else, for that matter) can be expected.

- **Costs** Sadly, unless you're prepared to subsist on a basic Afican diet, Mali - land-locked, relatively poor and with an effective hard currency - is an expensive country to visit. Remote Timbuktu is the most pricey place, due to its popularity with stubborn tourists and its genuine inaccessibility. Petrol costs a fortune here. As you near Bamako, linked to Dakar on the west coast by rail, prices drop and available commodities increase a little.

- **Desert Pistes** At the moment (summer 1995) the entire north of Mali, including Timbuktu and the southern half of the Tanezrouft piste, is still closed to outsiders. Following broken promises after the coup of 1990 the Tuareg, operating from the Adrar des Iforhas highlands are in revolt and causing sporadic havoc in the Tuareg homelands. The security situation has improved but the area may still be inaccessible. From Algeria, the only way into Mali is via Niger, but Tuareg rebels have also been operating on the Hoggar trans-Sahara route, robbing tourists right down to their underpants or even shooting them. While the Tuareg are unlikely to steal a motorcycle, you should not travel alone in the areas mentioned.

Despite these drawbacks, sub-Saharan Mali is a wonderful country of smiles, waves and colour that is well worth visiting, even if you can't get to the desert bits. There's no problem getting there via Mauritania (and Senegal) – see the *Rough Guide to West Africa* for the latest details. For the record, the southern half of the Tanezrouft is much rougher and more varied than the monotonous Algerian section. Further south, the track is either badly corrugated or very sandy, but there are wells in the very poor villages along the way. From Bourem, an exhausting, rutted sandy track follows the north bank of the Niger river to legendary Timbuktu. And if you still want more, try the piste that goes from Bamako to Kayes and ultimately Senegal (along the railway line). It is certainly not a desert piste, nor is it the short cut it appears to be, but it provides a fascinating (and complicated) slog through light jungle and rural Malian villages. This is back-roads West Africa at its best.

MAURITANIA

- **Capital** Nouakchott

- **Population** 2 million. 60% Moor, 40% Pulaar and other black ethnic groups.

- **Languages** Hassaniya (archaic Arabic), French. In the black south, Fula, Wolof and Solinke are spoken.

- **Visas** are required by all Europeans except French and Italians. If you're getting your visa on the way out, apply in Madrid (see Useful Addresses), not Rabat, which is not issuing them at present without showing a return air ticket.

- **Consulates** in Nouakchott. The nearest British representation is in Dakar, although the French (at rue Ahmed Ould Mahmed - B P. 231, ☎251 740) or US. Embassy may help you. Other embassies, all in the more prosperous northern half of the tiny capital, include those of Algeria and Senegal. There is no Mali consulate but you may be issued with a pass at the border to enter Mali.

The Atlantic Route to West Africa

Since problems in Algeria make traversing the two trans–Saharan routes in that country risky at the very least, the seemingly logical route along the Atlantic edge of the Sahara from the southern Morocco to Mauritania and Senegal has slowly come into use.

The Mauritanians have grudgingly allowed trans–Saharan traffic, including motor tourists, through their country by keeping land crossings across the Sahara possible. It is now the principal route for most overland trucking companies. At present (summer 1995) the coast road down to Dakhla in southern Morocco is straightforward. From here the military lead convoys of vehicles heading south to the Mauritanian border, leaving every Tuesday and Friday. It is not a particularly scenic part of the Sahara, with low cliffs keeping the piste off the beach. After about 350km the tarmac ends and the convoy passes through a sandy mine-field and continues to the Mauritanian border.

Nouadhibou is a Mauritanian port where you undertake entry formalities. If you arrive here without a visa you'll probably be turned back. There is a railway heading inland from the coast to the phosphate mines in northern Mauritania. It's possible to put your bike (or any other vehicle) on this train as far as Choum, close to Atar. The journey takes 14 hours and costs around UM2000 and trains leave every few days. If you travel on the open wagons it costs you nothing but you'll be black with phosphate dust by the time you get to Choum. The piste alongside the railway is very sandy, too much so to be a regular track.

Heading south from Nouadhibou you can also hook up with a private convoy which heads down the beach for the two day run to Nouakchott. A guide is essential for the north-ern section of this route. As more and more travellers come this way, more spurious guides will vie with the genuine ones for the fee, so be aware of this. From Nouakchott a sealed road continues down to Senegal or inland to Nema and thence northwestern Mali.

Returning from Mauritania to Morocco may be difficult as, officially, there is no exit north from Nouadhibou, but this may have changed by now.

- **Border Formalities** Don't count on getting away without a carnet (see Desert Documents). Fill out currency and valuables' declaration form, then report to Police at the first major town. If coming up from Nara in Mali, via Adel Bagrou, then you report to the Police in Nema, where you can also change money at the bank. Motor insurance did not seem necessary in 1990, but this may have been an oversight, so ask first.

- **Currency** About 180 ouguiya (UM) = £1. It's not exportable or available abroad (officially). You may be briefly searched for concealed 'oogs' when you leave the country.

- **Accommodation** Tourists are virtually unknown in Mauritania, although the growth of trans-Saharan traffic via the coast will have changed things marginally. Most hotels in the capital are in the business class and there is no campsite. Free camping too close to the capital and on the beach is likely to upset the jumpy security forces. Out in the country, asking around for a hotel or rooms may well result in being put up at a friendly local. Muslim nomad hospitality to strangers and travellers is renowned but do not take it for granted.

- **Costs** Imported goods are dear in Mauritania, but the fact that they even get there at all is due to the country's receipt of generous foreign aid from Saudi Arabia, the EEC and United States. Everything except ground-nuts, iron ore, sand and a little fresh produce is imported. Most tiny general stores or *boutiques* have a surprising range of dusty tinned and dried goods.

- **Desert Pistes** You'll need to team up with a car or two if you hope to follow the ancient trading route along the base of the Dhar Tichit, from Oualata to Tidjikja. A guide is essential as there are rarely any tracks and no *balises*. Ask for the venerable Nani in Nema, if he's still alive. There is much fascinating history along this route, which follows the ancient sites of the fishermen who once lived along the former Lake Aouker, now full of dunes. Make the most of it; you will probably only come here once and you won't see any other tourists.

The piste north to Chinguetti and the mountainous Adrar region, accessible from Tidjikja in the south, also requires a guide and is reputedly easier when ridden south to north, involving descent of dune slip faces rather than ascent See Travels in Mauritania by Peter Hudson and Impossible Journey by Michael Asher for a brief description of this route by camel. The northern route to or from Bir Mogrein to Tindouf in Algeria is reportedly open with Polisario (the freedom fighting remnants of what was Spanish Sahara) permission but don't count on it, especially coming up from the south. *Wüstenfahrer* (see Useful Addresses), have apparently got in and out of Mauritania via Bir Mogrein, but their tours come inland from Layoune on the former Spanish Saharan coast.

The coastal route north from the capital (in parts tidal) to the iron ore port of Nouadhibou requires a permit and is not as straightforward as it looks. It would be best to follow a supply lorry. From Nouadhibou you are advised to put your bike on to the empty ore train returning to the mines at Zouerat, as the piste alongside the track is very sandy all the way to Choum and there is a possibility of old Polisario War mines in this area as well as the southern end of former Spanish Sahara. The ore train is free to passengers who choose to travel on the uncovered wagons.

You will find Mauritanians to be an ideal balance between taciturn Arabs and sometimes over–gregarious black West Africans. Women are, socially at least, much more liberated, which makes a delightful change from neighbouring Algeria where they are rarely seen.

MOROCCO

- **Capital** Rabat.

- **Population** 24 million, 90% Berber, 10% Arab.

- **Languages** Arabic, French, Berber.

- **Visas** Not required for British citizens.

- **Consulates and Embassies in Rabat include**; Algeria (also in Oujda) Mauritania, Senegal, Ivory Coast. British Embassy is at 17 Blvd. de la Tour (☎20905/6).

- **Border Formalities** Green Cards are valid in Morocco, otherwise you have to leave your vehicle at the border to buy insurance in town. If entering from Figuig in Algeria this may mean a day's bus ride to Oujda to buy insurance. Note that frontiers between Algeria at Oujda and Figuig are sometimes closed without warning.

- **Currency** Dirham not sold officially out of the country. 16 Dh = £1.

- **Accommodation** Most of the main towns and cities in Morocco have campsites and, compared to its neighbours, there are many hotels at a reasonable cost. In the southern desert you can camp where you wish, as long as you are discreet.

- **Costs** By Saharan standards Morocco is well-geared towards European tourists, and is probably the cheapest to visit of all the countries mentioned here.

- **Desert Pistes** For those not wishing to commit themselves fully to the deep Sahara, Morocco offers a string of pistes along the southern edge of the High Atlas Mountains. From Tata in the west, near the Atlantic resort of Agadir, many pistes continue through Zagora to Erfoud and up to the eastern Moroccan Atlas. If riding in this area, take great care not to stray too far south to the disputed border with Algeria. The Michelin maps of this area (969 and 953) don't actually show the frontier, although the prohibited or truncated tracks shown do indicate the zone of contention. Dust Trails (see Useful Addresses) know this area very well and may be able to advise you on some good pistes.

NIGER

- **Capital** Niamey.

- **Population** 75 million, 50% Hausa, 20% Songhai and Djerma, 10% Fula, 10% Tuareg. The remainder are Kanouri and Beri Beri, or Bli Bli in the east.

- **Languages** Hausa is the most widely spoken, with Djerma and the Tuareg tongue of Tamachek also spoken. French is widely understood, but if you are staying in this area long it would be interesting to learn at least some Hausa, the lingua franca around these parts.

- **Visas** Not required by British citizens.

- **Consulates in Niamey include**; France (which deals with many West African visas), Algeria, Mali, Libya and US. The nearest UK representation is now in Dakar or Abidjan (Ivory Coast).

- **Border Formalities** At Assamaka, the only northern entry point, expect a little exploitation and much waiting around. Border guards anywhere can see that bikers haven't got much to give away and usually pick on cars. Buy a laissez passer. Motor insurance can be bought for the entire CFA zone saving you money and hassle in the long run. Once in the country, a delightful, colourful contrast compared to monochrome Algeria, you have to check in and out of every town, even if you are just passing by, for example at Tahoua. This process takes up many pages of your passport and is a chore unless you like meeting policemen.

- **Currency** CFA west. (See Mali currency)

- **Accommodation** You can camp where you like as long as you are ten miles away from any settlements (or well away from officials). As with Mali, campsites and hotels exist only in larger towns and the capital. Agadez has plenty of both. Once you shake off the authorities, the local people are often most generous, curious and helpful.

- **Costs** Not quite as expensive as in some parts of Mali. Niger's uranium reserves at Arlit and its economic co-operation with France (which covets the aforementioned product) give the capital quite a sophisticated feel, with plenty of imported goods on offer. Petrol is similar to the UK price, apart from in the border town of Birni-Nkonni. Here you will be all but dragged off your bike by thirteen-year olds with jerricans offering you black market, Nigerian petrol (very cheap there) for sale. Keep your wits about you, and watch out for set-ups or watered-down fuel. On a bike, you might save yourself £10-15 if you are nearly empty and are prepared to drive a hard bargain.

- **Desert Pistes** The trouble with Niger is that apart from the 200km section of the trans–Sahara route from Arlit to Assamaka, you can't (officially) ride on any unsealed track without an expensive guide. On a bike this is obviously a problem, but it is not insoluble.

- **For those determined** to ride the pistes of the beautiful Aïr Mountains and Ténéré Desert beyond. Try to get to know one of the Agadez-based tour companies operating 4WDs in the Ténéré region. Agence Temet Voyages (see Useful Addresses) are one of the most experienced and even offer 4x4 supported motorbike tours in the Ténéré (You can guess which bike they provide...). It won't be cheap - the official fee for a group guide is £30/day - but it would be the chance of a lifetime short of joining one of the German adventure bike tour companies (see Useful Addresses following the Temet Voyages entry).

- **The route south** from Agadez to Zinder may be completely sealed by now, and does not require a guide, but a permit may be necessary, so ask first. The need for a guide is not just a way of getting more money out of tourists with an extravagant taste for adventure. Over the years enough people (including experienced locals) have gone missing in the Ténéré to make travelling with a guide mandatory.

TUNISIA

Tunisia may be great for suntans and windsurfing but has little to offer the adventurous off-road biker other than a handy route to Algeria's eastern pistes. The south of Tunisia is a military area. Touzeur - El Oued is the main desert crossing to Algeria and Ben Gardane on the coast, the way into Libya.

PERSONAL CONDUCT

THE FOLLOWING GUIDELINES all boil down to respecting local laws, customs and sensibilities. Many of them derive from the mores of Islam which, like other oriental religions, is much more a 'way of life' than Christianity is in the West. Islam has great respect for Christianity, with which it shares many of its early myths; Jesus Christ himself is mentioned as a prophet in the Koran, Islam's Holy Book. However, devote Moslems will be contemptuous of anyone who denies the existence of a God. Therefore, if you are the fortunate recipient of Moslem hospitality, it is best to swallow any atheistic principles you may hold dear and call yourself a Christian, or whatever, when the topic turns towards religion, as it may well do.

There is a certain fear about transgressing social etiquette when dealing with Moslems and Arabs. This can make an extended stay among traditional Arabs of a high status a nerve-racking experience. The 'left hand' rule is commonly known. Moslems find our use of toilet paper as disgusting as we find their use of the left hand for the same purpose. However, there is no need to become paranoid about such things. By observing and mimicking the behaviour of your host or those around you, you are unlikely to cause intentional offence. Contrary to impressions, people do not struggle to perform daily tasks one-handed; like many taboos, this one has its roots in common, hygienic sense. Another anticipated ceremony is the preparation and drinking of sweet, mint tea in tiny glasses. Nomadic lore suggests that the offer of a third glass is a signal to make your farewells and move on, failure of which would cause gross offence (or, more likely, inconvenience). The truth is, you can drink as much or as little of the delicious, sweet tea as you wish. Any offers of further hospitality will be made clear without recourse to obscure rituals.

Many of the guidelines listed below are a matter of common sense, with many of the most strict taboos only observed in the devout regions of the more fundamentalist countries. Living in the Sahara is hard enough and, especially amongst desert nomads, the interpretation of Islamic law tends to be pragmatic rather than dogmatic.

- For even the most perfunctory exchange, always introduce yourself to strangers with a greeting and a handshake.

• Men should not talk to, touch or even look at women unless they approach you.

• Do not touch other people, pass things or eat with your left hand.

• During Ramadan (a month of daytime abstinence similar to Christians' Lent) do not eat, drink, smoke or otherwise enjoy yourself in public during daylight hours. In 1996, Ramadan will begin on January 25th, and approximately 10 days earlier in each subsequent year. When Ramadan falls during the long days of summer months, people get a bit cranky.

• Unlike neighbouring Morocco, hashish is an especially heavy bust in sober Algeria. Possession of harder drugs will carry stiff, even terminal sentences elsewhere on the continent.

• The Moslem 'weekend' begins on Thursday, with Friday being the day of prayer. Shops and other services close at midday on Thursday and reopen on Saturday morning.

• While in the desert, or at campsites, you may dress as you wish but whatever the weather, dress conservatively in towns. To Moslems the sight of a bare body is either offensive or unequivocally provocative.

• Always ask people first if you may take their photograph or film them. This is a typical area of tourist insensitivity. Disregarding the belief that photography steals the subject's soul, consider the rudeness of being photographed as an 'exotic local' while walking down your own High Street.

ITINERARIES IN THE SAHARA

THESE ARE SOME OF THE PISTES I have done over the past few years With the exception of H2. They are all within the scope of a first time visitor to the Sahara, and any difficulties, if present, have been clearly explained. The information and descriptions were collated from memory, notes and photographs, as well as from reference to the commonly used maps and the French, German and English guide books available (see Books section).

Be aware of current conditions. At present (summer 1995) routes F, I, J and K are still closed or restricted due to Tuareg incursions in these areas. It is your responsibility to ascertain the situation in each area as accurately as possible before you leave. The embassies and tourist offices of the country in question are unreliable. The Foreign Office Travel Desk (☎0171 270 4129) can give you the official view (usually "stay at home"), but much more detailed information can be obtained from overland tour companies that travel in the area, or from experts like Ken Slavin at K&J Slavin Quest in Lincolnshire (☎01507 313401); Duncan Gough of D. Gough Ltd in Wiltshire (☎01373 858272); or even myself, via the Travellers' Bookshop in London.

Algerian Desert Pistes

B. Ghardaia – Tamanrasset.	1303km
C. Ghardaia – Illizi.	1282km
D. Illizi – Djanet	400km
E. Djanet – Tamanrasset (via Assekrem)	660km
F. Tamanrasset – Bordj Moktar	714km

Hoggar Mountain Pistes

H1. Tamanrasset- Assekrem – Tamanrasset	180km
H2. Hirhafok – In Amguel	70km
H3. Ideles – Tahifet - Tamanrasset	207km

Trans–Saharan Pistes

I. Reggane – Gao	1368km
J. Tamanrasset – Arlit	655km
K Bourem – Timbuktu	330km

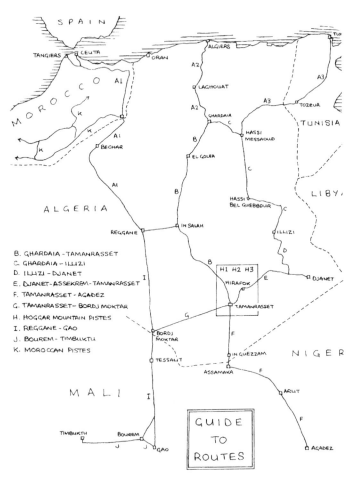

B. GHARDAIA - TAMANRASSET
C. GHARDAIA - ILLIZI
D. ILLIZI - DJANET
E. DJANET - ASSEKREM - TAMANRASSET
F. TAMANRASSET - AGADEZ
G. TAMANRASSET - BORDJ MOKTAR
H. HOGGAR MOUNTAIN PISTES
I. REGGANE - GAO
J. BOUREM - TIMBUKTU
K. MOROCCAN PISTES

GUIDE TO ROUTES

© 1991
P. CORBETT

ROUTE B: GHARDAIA – TAMANRASSET

Distance. 1303km – 814 miles.

Road conditions. By now the tarmac should be completely repaired, but expect diversions off the road at any time and potholes in the older sections of tarmac.

Fuel. From Ghardaia southwards you should think twice about passing a petrol station without filling up. There are stations at Ghardaia, Hassi-Fahl, El Golea, In Salah, Arak, In Ecker and Tamanrasset. The longest fuel-less stretch is the 400km from El Golea to In Salah: the Tademait plateau.

Water. Available at petrol stations or in towns.

Maps. Recommended: Michelin 953. Useful: IGN I:Im sheets NH31, NG31, NF31.

Route Description

Route finding all the way to Tamanrasset is straightforward in good conditions as by now, the road should be fully repaired all the way with no long diversions.

From Ghardaia, ride out of the valley and head south along the tarmac road. After 24km you pass the left turn for Ouargla and, ultimately, Djanet, and after 110km you pass the petrol station at Hassi–Fahl. At a signpost indicating 'El Golea/El Meniaa 120' you are right in a striking area of dunes, a popular place for photographs. As you near El Golea the road begins to twist, watch out for sand drifts. Once in El Golea, you'll find a baker and market on the east side of the centrally divided main street. Southeast of the town is the thousand year-old fort of El Meniaa after which the town has been re-named. The petrol station is to the south of town.

Leaving El Golea, past the sand rose vendors, the road takes the first step up to the Tademait plateau. Sixty five kilometres south of El Golea is the junction for road to the west, and 105km from town, after the final rise onto the true Tademait, is a corrugated piste to Fort Mirabel (known locally as Chebaba), 15km to the southeast. It has a well and used to be a popular camping spot for the overland trucking companies, since the fort, unlike some, is still intact and clean.

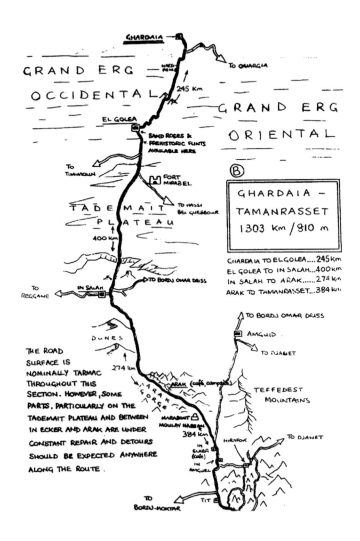

GHARDAIA

HASSI FAHL

TO OUARGLA

GRAND ERG OCCIDENTAL

245 Km

GRAND ERG ORIENTAL

EL GOLEA

SAND ROSES & PREHISTORIC FLINTS AVAILABLE HERE

TO TIMIMOUN

FORT MIRABEL

TADEMAIT PLATEAU

TO HASSI BEL GUEBBOUR

400 km

TO BORDJ OMAR DRISS

IN SALAH

TO REGGANE

Ⓑ

GHARDAIA —
TAMANRASSET

1303 km / 810 m

GHARDAIA TO EL GOLEA....245 km
EL GOLEA TO IN SALAH...400 km
IN SALAH TO ARAK......274 km
ARAK TO TAMANRASSET...384 km

TO BORDJ OMAR DRISS

AMGUID

TO DJANET

DUNES

THE ROAD SURFACE IS NOMINALLY TARMAC THROUGHOUT THIS SECTION. HOWEVER, SOME PARTS, PARTICULARLY ON THE TADEMAIT PLATEAU AND BETWEEN IN ECKER AND ARAK ARE UNDER CONSTANT REPAIR AND DETOURS SHOULD BE EXPECTED ANYWHERE ALONG THE ROUTE.

274 km

ARAK (café, campsite)

ARAK GORGE

TEFFEDEST MOUNTAINS

MARABOUT MOULAY HASSAN

384 km

HIRAFOK

TO DJANET

IN ECKER (café)

IN AMGUEL

TO BORDJ-MOKTAR

TIT

You may come across one or two roadhouses an the Tademait Plateau but otherwise it is a bleak and windy place to stop on. Descending steeply off the plateau, 312km from El Golea, In Salah is a little over an hour away. The narrow road drops through some sandy patches, past outlying remnants of the Tademait, to the perennial sand drifts within sight of the town. The petrol station is on the main road which bypasses In Salah, while the campsite is on the west side of town, under the encroaching dunes. Halfway to Arak you will pass straw-coloured dune ranges on either side of the road. Two hundred and sixty four kilometres from In Salah you turn east and enter the Arak Gorge where, after l0km, you come across a petrol station/cafe/campsite. Continuing south, the gorge flattens out into low, rounded hills. A hundred and ten kilometres from Arak is the tomb of Moulay Lahsene, a holy man who died here on his way to Mecca; superstitious lore requires that you ride round the tomb three times for good luck. This is an area of unusual, eroded boulders. Two hundred and ten kilometres from Arak is In Ecker, where there's another petrol station. Tamanrasset is now 200km away, past the Tuareg villages of In Amguel, Tit and Outoul. On arrival in Tamanrasset, ride straight through the busy town centre to the expensive Hotel Tahat, or the Zeribas campsite on the town's southeastern edge.

ROUTE C: GHARDAIA – ILLIZI

Distance. 1282 km – 801 miles.

Road conditions. Sealed tarmac all the way, but expect potholes, sand on the road and diversions.

Fuel. Available at Ghardaia, Ouargla, Hassi Messaoud, Draa El Baguel, Hassi bel Guebbour, In Amenas and Illizi.

Water. Available from petrol stations along the route but always carry a large reserve.

Maps. Recommended: Michelin 953. Useful IGN l:lm sheet NH32.

Route Description.

Twenty four kilometres south of Ghardaia turn east for the oil towns of Ouargla and Hassi Messaoud. From here, head south along the natural corridor or '*gassi*' which divides the dunes of the Grand Erg Oriental. About 120km from Hassi Messaoud there is a petrol station at Draa El

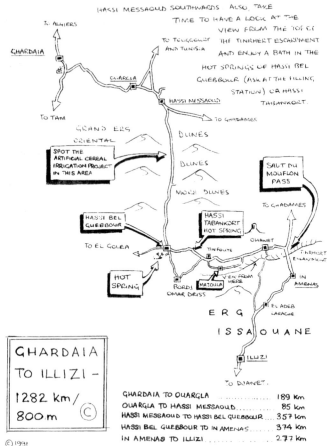

THIS ROUTE SHOULD BE ALL TARMAC, DOMINATED
BY MAJOR OIL TOWNS. LOOK OUT FOR POTHOLES FROM
HASSI MESSAOUD SOUTHWARDS. ALSO, TAKE
TIME TO HAVE A LOOK AT THE
VIEW FROM THE TOP OF
THE TINRHERT ESCARPMENT
AND ENJOY A BATH IN THE
HOT SPRINGS OF HASSI BEL
GUEBBOUR (ASK AT THE FILLING
STATION) OR HASSI
TABANKORT.

TO ALGIERS

GHARDAIA

TO TOUGGOURT
AND TUNISIA

OUARGLA

HASSI MESSAOUD

TO GHADAMES

TO TAM

GRAND ERG
ORIENTAL

DUNES

SPOT THE
ARTIFICIAL CEREAL
IRRIGATION PROJECT
IN THIS AREA

DUNES

SAUT DU
MOUFLON
PASS

MORE DUNES

TO GHADAMES

HASSI BEL
GUEBBOUR

HASSI
TABANKORT
HOT SPRING

OUANET

TO EL GOLEA

TIN FOUYE

TINRHERT
ESCARPMENT

HOT
SPRING

VIEW FROM
HERE

BORDJ
OMAR DRISS

MAJOULA

IN
AMENAS

ERG

EL ADEB
LARACHE

ISSA OUANE

ILLIZI

GHARDAIA
TO ILLIZI —
1282 km/
800 m   (C)

TO DJANET.

GHARDAIA TO OUARGLA .... 189 Km
OUARGLA TO HASSI MESSAOUD .... 85 Km
HASSI MESSAOUD TO HASSI BEL GUEBBOUR .... 357 Km
HASSI BEL GUEBBOUR TO IN AMENAS .... 374 Km
IN AMENAS TO ILLIZI .... 277 Km

Playing in the dunes near Hassi bel Guebbour, Algeria. Great
fun but risky. (M. Spencer)

Baguel, while on the other side of the road are rosy dunes, well worth
climbing for a view of the impenetrable erg beyond. South of here you
may come across the extraordinary sight of bright green grass with a
backdrop of massive dunes, some kind of artesian irrigation project.

At Hassi bel Guebbour, basically a petrol station, cafe and junction
of routes, the tarmac turns east towards Ohanet. There are a couple of
warm springs nearby, handy for a wash, one is just a kilometre along the
Bordj Omar Driss road, surrounded by tall reeds and popular with passing drivers. Nearby is a cache of bike tyres which we buried in '89 and
never collected; if you can find them, they're yours. The other spring is
61km from 'HbG' along the Ohanet road, signposted as 'Hassi
Tabankort', and found a few minutes ride north of the road.

Anywhere after the oil installations at Tin Fouye, a short ride southwards across the gravel will bring you to the edge of the Tinrhert
escarpment and a view over the barren plain to the Erg Issaouane and
the western Tassili. 50km past Ohanet, after a right turn, the road
descends 200m down to the desert from the Saut de Mouflon Pass.
Continue on to In Amenas, an oil town with the usual essentials of
bread, water and fuel. Illizi is 280km to the south, along a new road
which passes through some beautiful dunescapes. If heading for Djanet
you must check out with the Police at Illizi

ROUTE D: ILLIZI - DJANET

Distance. 400km – 250 miles.

Piste conditions. Immediately south of Illizi there is a wide corrugated piste and, later, a few sandy oued crossings. On the Fadnoun Plateau the track traverses bare rock and is mostly corrugated, but this is no problem (in fact it's great fun!) on a trail bike. From Zaoutallaz (as it is marked on the '953' map) or Bordj El Haouas (as it is now known), the piste to Djanet is thoroughly corrugated, but with low tyre pressures you'll get a smoother ride on the sand either side of the piste. The main road in Djanet (and to the airport) is sealed.

Fuel. Available at Illizi, possibly at Zaouatallaz, and at Djanet.

Water. Available at Illizi, Iherir (25km off-piste), Zaouatallaz and Djanet.

Maps. Essential: IGN I:Im sheet NG32. Useful: Michelin 953.

Route Description

The piste is a clear track right across the Fadnoun Plateau up to Bordj El Haouas (Zaouatallaz) and southeast to Djanet. This is one of the most spectacular and varied of Algeria's popular pistes.

In Illizi, turn right at the fort and follow the corrugated piste through the shanty town that has sprung up since work began on the tarmac road to Djanet. At present, Djanet is supplied by lorries that cannot cross the Fadnoun and have to come from Hassi bel Guebbour via Amguid.

A couple of kilometres from Illizi is the branch east to Tarat, near the Libyan border, an intriguing piste that requires a guide, available in Illizi. The IGN NG32 map clearly indicates where the piste dips steeply into a couple of dried valleys before the major descent at Gara Inhadja N'Kli. From the top of the pass (125km from Illizi) you can clearly see the many deviations which have developed in an attempt to avoid the horrible corrugations on the plain below. It's a good place not to be in a Series III Land Rover! One hundred and seventy kilometres from Illizi there is a fork right (known as the 'Afara piste') which leads to the Amguid-Djanet truck piste and provides a marginally quicker route to Tamanrasset. As the '953' indicates, this is a 'picturesque stretch of road'.

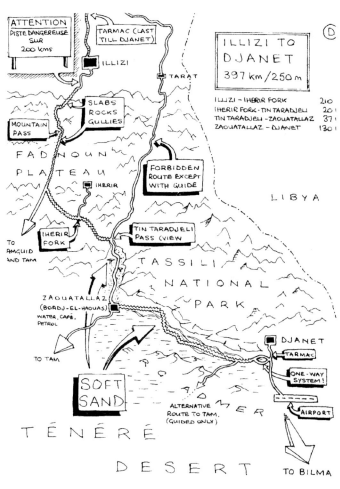

ATTENTION
PISTE DANGEREUSE
SUR
200 kms

TARMAC (LAST
TILL DJANET)

ILLIZI

TARAT

Ⓓ

ILLIZI TO
DJANET
397 km / 250 m

ILLIZI – IHERIR FORK	210
IHERIR FORK – TIN TARADJELI	20
TIN TARADJELI – ZAOUATALLAZ	37
ZAOUATALLAZ – DJANET	130

SLABS
ROCKS
GULLIES

MOUNTAIN
PASS

FAD N O U N

P L A T E A U

IHERIR

FORBIDDEN
ROUTE EXCEPT
WITH GUIDE

L I B Y A

IHERIR
FORK

TO
AMGUID
AND TAM

TIN TARADJELI
PASS (VIEW

T A S S I L I

N A T I O N A L

ZAOUATALLAZ
(BORDJ-EL-HAOUAS)
WATER, CAFÉ,
PETROL

P A R K

DJANET

TARMAC

ONE-WAY
SYSTEM!

TO TAM

SOFT
SAND

ALTERNATIVE
ROUTE TO TAM.
(GUIDED ONLY)

M E R

AIRPORT

T É N É R É

D E S E R T

TO BILMA

© 1991
P. CORBETT

Beyond the fork, the corrugations improve slightly and 210km from Illizi is an Arabic sign indicating the steep, rocky piste down to the unspoilt and isolated Tuareg village of Iherir, 25km to the north. In the guelta (rock pool) near Iherir, the last Saharan dwarf crocodile was caught in the 1920s. Back on the main route, after another 20km you struggle through a sandy gorge to the spectacular pass at Tin Taradjeli. Here the piste finally descends to the desert floor, continuing through a broadening valley dotted with trees to Bordj El Haouas. Here there's a cafe with water, possibly a police check and possibly fuel. You may also be charged a hefty £10 fee for entering the Tassili N'Ajjer National Park. From Bordj El Haouas, a corrugated and sometimes sandy piste leads to Djanet, 130km to the southeast. With the Tassili crags to the north and the dunes of the Erg Admer to the south, this is a breathtaking ride. Take your time to explore a little before moving on to Djanet and checking–in with the various authorities.

ROUTE E: DJANET – ASSEKREM – TAMANRASSET

Distance. 660km – 412 miles

Piste conditions. There's a wide corrugated track to Bordj El Haouas. From here to Ideles there are occasional soft patches or longer sandy sections along oueds, as well as the usual corrugations. From Hirhafok the mountain track that leads to the Assekrem turn-off is steep and can be washed-out in places. Continuing down to Tamanrasset, the wide track is badly corrugated.

Fuel. Available at Djanet and Tamanrasset. Don't count on fuel at Bordj El Haouas or Ideles. You must carry an enormous amount of fuel for this route but, on the bright side, your bike loses about 5kg every 50 miles as the fuel gets used up.

Water. Available at Djanet, Bordj El Haouas, Ideles and the Hoggar villages. There are no usable wells along the middle part of this route.

Maps. Essential: IGN l:lm sheet NG32. Recommended: IGNl:lm NF31, US DMA. sheet TPCH3-D. Useful: Michelin 953.

FROM THE 'TAM' DRUM TO HIRAFOK, MOST OF THIS ROUTE IS CORRUGATED. FROM IDELES OR HIRAFOK SOUTHWARDS, THE PISTE IS VERY STEEP AND ROCKY.

SHORT CUT AT YOUR PERIL!!

TAM VIA TIRIRINE (GUIDE ESSENTIAL)

SEROUENOUT (NO WATER)

VIEW FROM SEROUENOUT FORT

OUED PISTE / ALT. PISTE

OUED PISTE / ALT. PISTE

ALTERNATIVE PISTE

TO AMGUID & ILLIZI

TO ILLIZI

ADRAR RANGE

OIL DRUM (BORNE)

TAZAT

ZAOUATALLAZ

ERG ADMER

DJANET

TO LIBYA

TASSILI N'AJJER

TELERHEBA

IDELES

TAZROUK

TAHIFET

DJANET VIA TIRIRINE (WITH GUIDE)

TO SALAH

IN AMGUEL

HIRAFOK

ASSEKREM

TAMANRASSET

ATAKOR RANGE

TO IN GUEZZAM AND NIGER

TO BORDJ MOKTAR AND MALI

© 1991 P. CORBETT

DJANET TAMANRASSET 730 km / 455 m	
DJANET TO ZAOUATALLAZ	130 km
ZAOUATALLAZ TO 'TAM' DRUM	90 km
'TAM' DRUM TO SEROUENOUT	50 km
SEROUENOUT TO HIRAFOK	230 km
HIRAFOK TO ASSEKREM	75 km
ASSEKREM TO TAMANRASSET	85 km

Ⓔ

Route Description

The central section of this route may provide difficulties in orientation in conditions of poor visibility. If this is your first major piste, it is less stressful to complete it in convoy with other vehicles, at least as far as Ideles.

Check-out with the authorities in Djanet and return the 130km to Bordj El Haouas. Fill up with fuel if you can, as it's still over 500km to Tamanrasset, your next guaranteed fuel supply. The short-cut that the IGN NG-32 map suggests (missing out Bordj') will more likely mean getting stuck or disorientated in the Oued Bourahla or adjacent boulder field. It's best to at least get in sight of Bordj' before turning south. Fifteen kilometres after Bordj El Haouas, the piste turns southwest and crosses a couple of dried–up river courses. To the west the distinctive peak of Mount Tazat (2165m) appears. Follow the piste around the south of the mountain, past some dunes and the occasional metal marker post, to the piste junction marked 'Borne' on the Michelin 953 map or, with the spot height of '1094' on the IGN NG-32 map. Here the truck piste continues WNW (an abbreviation for 'west-north-west' or about 292°) to Amguid while a less clear branch turns SSW to Fort Serouenout and the Hoggar. This junction is marked by a beaten-up orange oil drum which once supported a signpost. The two metre high balises leading on to Amguid are visible, but those leading to Serouenout and Tamanrasset are only barely so. It is common to over anticipate the orange oil drum and become anxious when it does not appear when expected. With careful attention to the IGN map, distances and landmarks (such as Mount Tazat) the drum should appear 90km from Bordj El Haouas. By following the clearest tracks to the southwest east you will soon pick up cairns and marker posts stamped 'TAM' and not 'AM' (for Amguid) - another possible source of confusion.

Before you get to the fort at Serouenout, there are some sandy sections to negotiate, particularly at the crossing of the Oued Tafassasset and by the old Simca wreck. The graffiti-ridden rubbish dump of Fort Serouenout appears 270km from Djanet (or 50km from the drum). Used as a toilet, and with the polluted wells now capped, this is a far cry from a Beau Geste romantic fantasy. Looking west from the fort is a flat-topped hill. To the right (north) is an alternative piste that rejoins the old route about 120km further on, past Mount Telertheba. The old piste, which is more interesting and a little more difficult to ride (but straightforward to follow) continues south of the flat-topped hill through narrow, sandy valleys dotted with occasional thorn trees. Mount Telertheba appears as a ridge of jagged peaks to the south. There is an area of very soft, powdery, grey sand about 360km from Djanet, with Telertheba over your left shoulder. Be ready to blast through this obstacle as riding slowly or stopping usually means getting stuck or falling off. The piste in this area is crossed by shallow drainage channels from the mountains, which can reduce the speed of bikes with limited suspension travel.

Further on, as the piste continues southwest across a plain, odd eroded plinths topped with thorn trees appear, making handy windbreaks for an evening camp. Corrugations reappear as you near the Hoggar foothills, where the piste turns into a single track, rising, dipping and twisting over oueds and volcanic rubble to the village of Ideles. The corrugated piste by-passes the town and a couple of kilometres later the track splits for Tahifet (see route H3) 467km from Djanet. Turn right for Hirhafok. The piste is wide and fast as you ride through Tuareg gardens concentrated along the oueds. Passing a turning right to Mertoutek (and ultimately Amguid) you arrive at the village of Hirhafok, 500km from Djanet. You can carry on straight for In Amguel and the highway, 90km to the west (see route H2), but a marginally shorter, and infinitely more exhilarating piste turns left through the village for the Atakor, the spectacular core of the Hoggar massif.

Thirty five kilometres from Hirhafok, along a winding mountain track, you will pass by the gueltas of Issakarassene on the right (west) of the piste.

From here onwards, the track steepens through washed-out gullies up to the col at Tin Teratimt. Not all cars can manage the ascent to the pass but you should be fine on a trail bike. Down off the Col, you come to the turning for Assekrem, 70km from Hirhafok. A steep and rocky 5km ride brings you to the pass at Assekrem. Here Foucauld's famous hermitage is still occupied by monks from his Order, Les Petits Frères de Foucauld. Although sometimes crowded (a relative term in the Sahara) the magnificent view from Assekrem over the peaks below is a sight not to be missed, especially at sunrise or sunset.

Returning the 5km to the junction, continue southwards along the wide and very corrugated piste to Tamanrasset, 80km away. Fifteen kilometres before Tamanrasset is Jojo's spring, an unrationed source of water and a possible camping alternative to Tam' itself.

ROUTE F: TAMANRASSET - BORDJ MOKTAR

Distance. 714km – 446 miles

Road conditions. Corrugations up to Abalessa and some stony sections to Silet. Smooth and fast up to the Oued Tamanrasset crossing just before Tlm Missao, and less so moving on south to Timiaouine. From Timia' to Bordj Moktar the track is badly corrugated.

Fuel. Available at Tamanrasset, possibly Silet and Timia and even Bordj Moktar is not guaranteed but here you would just have to wait or ask around.

Water. Tamanrasset, Abalessa, Silet, Tlm Missao (well), Tlmiaouine (well) and Bordj Moktar.

Maps. Essential: IGN 1:1m sheet NF31. Useful: Michelin 953.

The Tanezrouft piste looks like this for over 500 miles (A.Humphrey).

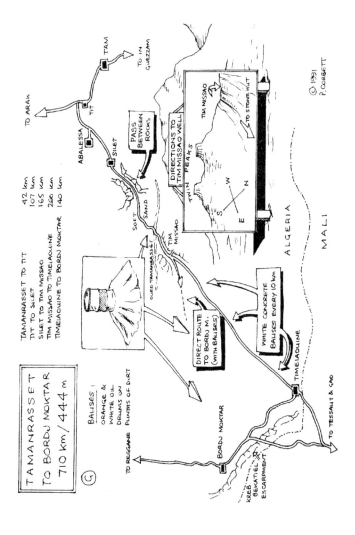

TO ARAK

TAM

TO IN GUEZZAM

TIT

ABALESSA

SILET

PASS BETWEEN ROCKS

DIRECTIONS TO TIM MISSAO WELL

TIM MISSAO

TO STONE HUT

TWIN PEAKS

N W S E

ALGERIA

MALI

© 1991
P. CORBETT

TAMANRASSET TO TIT	42 Km
TIT TO SILET	107 Km
SILET TO TIM MISSAO	165 Km
TIM MISSAO TO TIMEIAOUINE	260 Km
TIMEIAOUINE TO BORDJ MOKTAR	140 Km

SOFT SAND

OUED TAMANRASSET

TIM MISSAO

DIRECT ROUTE TO BORDJ M. (WITH BALISES)

WHITE CONCRETE BALISES EVERY 10 Km

TIMEIAOUINE

TO TESSALIT & GAO

TAMANRASSET TO BORDJ MOKTAR 710 Km / 444 m

BALISES:
ORANGE & WHITE OIL DRUMS ON PLINTHS OF DIRT

TO REGGANE

BORDJ MOKTAR

KREB BEKRATIEL ESCARPMENT

Route Description

The piste is clear all the way to the well at Tim Missao, which can be difficult to find. Also, the orientation towards Timiaouine, a short distance west of Tlm Missao, can be confusing with the new *balises* (presumably - I have not continued in this direction) continuing directly WSW to Bordj.

Leave Tamanrasset and ride northwards along the tarmac highway. Just after the village of Tit, at a large stone block, turn left onto the corrugated track that leads to Abalessa. Here, the tomb of the ancestral Tuareg queen, Tin Hinan, was excavated in 1934. The nature of the tomb, and the artefacts discovered within, suggest that this may have been an extreme outpost of the Roman Empire. Leave Abalessa across a sandy oued and follow the rough track to Silet, 149km from Tamanrasset. Around here the hills begin to sink into the reg of the Tanezrouft. Check-out with the Police in Silet and leave the village to the northwest, although the route soon curves back to the southwest. From here onwards, the piste has now been marked with mounds of sand topped with red-and-white painted oil drums to aid navigation. Forty three kilometres from Silet you pass between the rocky outcrop of Adrar Isket, a good place for a sheltered and secluded camp. From Adrar Isket the piste is smooth and fast, following the course of the Oued Tamanrasset, distinct only as a thin line of sporadic vegetation. A hundred and forty kilometres from Silet you cross the grassy oued, near some dunes, and head directly southwest with the Adrar Timekerkaz hills emerging to the south. The landmarks for Tim Missao begin 20km from the oued crossing. Here, a stone hut (once site of an aerodrome) marks the point to head southeast for 5km to the twin buttresses clearly visible on the horizon (see map). The entrance to the well is through a valley to the right of the buttresses. Once in the valley, keep right, riding over a low dune into the small canyon of Tim Missao and its well. Ancient and modern graffiti covers the canyon walls and near here Henri Lhote, the late scholar of prehistoric Saharan art, discovered depictions of chariots. This suggests that horse-drawn chariots of the Romans or Garamantians (ancient Libyans) may have indeed crossed the Sahara to the Niger, via the Hoggar and Tassili. Further chariot engravings exist at Tademeka in the Adrar des Iforhas hills, only 300km from the river. In 1985 an American expedition finally discovered a pair of much sought-after chariot wheels at Tassili N'Eridjane, directly south of Tim Missao.

The red-and-white-oil drum mounds may (see above) continue directly to Bordj Moktar, but the established route, located sometimes with difficulty, continues south and southwest to Timiaouine. It's marked with metre–high, white concrete bollards indicating either 'Tlmia' or 'Silet' (depending on your direction), with the distance given in kilometres. The reg is flat and unremarkable all the way to Tlmia, With the exception of Pic Oul, to the south of the piste l00km from Tim Missao.

Timiaouine is 260km from Tlm Missao (about 580km from Tam'), and here you may be able to buy some petrol if your battery can activate the pumps or, more expensively, from anyone who will sell you some. There is also a well and a bakery, which sells delicious brown loaves - just follow your nose. After checking-out with the Police, leave town to the west and then follow the very corrugated track northwest to Bordj Moktar, l40km from Timia. Check-in and out with Police and also Customs if you're heading for Mali. There is usually fuel available and an expensive cafe at Bordj.

ROUTE H1: TAMANRASSET – ASSEKREM – TAMANRASSET

Distance. l80km –112 miles.

Piste conditions. Very corrugated and then steep up to Assekrem, less corrugated, but at times very steep and twisted, down to the Tuareg village of Terhenanet. From here the piste is occasionally sandy.

Fuel. Tamanrasset

Water. Available at Tamanrasset (water in Tam is only turned on between 8–l0am and 4–6pm) and at Jojo's spring (no restrictions). Also at gueltas off the route and at Terhenanet. There is rarely water to spare at Assekrem.

Maps. Recommended: IGN l:lm sheet NF3l, IGN l:200,000 sheets titled 'Tamanrasset' and 'Assekrem'.

Route description

The only difficulty, other than the steep descent from Assekrem, is finding the usual way back to the road at Outoul. For this reason this route is given in the easier, anticlockwise direction.

Turn off Tam's ring road (see town map) for Jojo's spring and Assekrem. Passing the distinctive trachyte plug of Iharen at 12km, the track begins to rise and soon becomes completely corrugated as it steepens towards Assekrem, 80km from town. At first there is little evidence of the spectacle ahead, as the piste winds its way up across a plateau of volcanic rubble.

About 60km from Tam you pass a track leading off to the south-east to the gueltas at Afilale. Fifteen kilometres later you reach the junction, where you should keep left for Assekrem. The right fork leads to Hirhafok via the Tin Teratimt Pass. The last 4km to Assekrem are very steep, rocky and. rutted by wheels scrabbling for traction. You may be charged an entrance or parking fee as you enter the saddle where Assekrem sits. There is a small lodge here, which caters for the tourist groups driven up from Tamanrasset. You may be able to eat and sleep at the lodge (at a price) if there is room. The steep walk up to the chapel and hermitage is what everyone comes for, and they come from all over the world, as the visitors' book in the tiny library testifies. It is an extraordinary place nearly 9000' high, in the middle of the Sahara.

Coming down the other side of the pass, you ride through stony, barren hillsides with the odd, cleared patch on which to camp. Seventeen kilometres from Assekrem you pass right by the peak of Ilamane, with its typical fluted columns of cooled, basaltic lava. From this point, the track descends in a series of steep drop-offs. This is clearly the less-travelled route to Assekrem and much more interesting for it.

Just past an area of boulders and soft sand, as the piste begins to level out, you ride through a brief patch of sand. It has consistency of glass beads, and can be very tricky on a bike; it's best blasted through under power, or walked across. The piste leads on through a oued to the Tuareg village of Terhenanet, about 35km from Assekrem, and from here continues southwards. Forty five kilometres after Terhenanet you cross the large Oued Otoul. From here it is easy to lose the main piste and end up regaining the highway through the peripheral buildings, pylons and storage sheds of Outoul. It doesn't really matter which way you go from here as the highway is only a short distance to the southwest. However, if attempting this route in the reverse (clockwise) direction, note that you should turn off the road 10km north of Tamanrasset, just after the airport, crossing the Oued Otoul 13km later.

ROUTE H2: HIRHAFOK-IN AMGUEL

Distance. 70km – 43 miles.

Piste conditions. A mildly corrugated sandy piste.

Fuel. There may be fuel at Ideles, 35km east of Hirhafok and at In Ecker, 35km north of In Amguel. Otherwise Tamanrasset is 125km south of In Amguel along the highway.

Water. Available at Hirhafok (well) and at In Amguel.

Maps. Useful: IGN I:lm sheet NF31, IGN 1:200,000 sheet titled 'Assekrem'.

Route description

This piste is easy to follow and ride. For the first half of the route it winds gently through the northern Hoggar foothills. The piste is wide, clear and relatively free of corrugations all the way to the highway. It actually rejoins the main highway a few kilometres south of In Amguel. From this point, it's 125km south to Tamanrasset along the tarmac road. This is the easiest way to end the run from Djanet if you are unable to face the drama of the Atakor.

ROUTE H3: IDELES – TAHIFET – TAMANRASSET

Distance. 207km –129 miles

Piste conditions. Corrugated at first, with sandy oued crossings, then long sections of sandy ruts.

Fuel. Ideles (possibly) and Tamanrasset.

Water. Available at Ideles, Tazrouk (27km off the route), Tahifet, In Dalag and Tarhaouhaout (both these last two villages are off the route) and at Tam.

Maps. Recommended: IGN I:lm sheet NF31, IGN 1:200,000 sheets titled 'Assekrem' and 'Tamanrasset' cover most of the route.

Route description

It is easy to get confused at the junction of the piste to Tazrouk, 50km from Ideles; the lesser used piste to the right is the one to follow for Tahifet and Tamanrasset. Other than this, the route is clear, with the use of your odometer and the IGN NF-31 'Tamanrasset' l:lm map.

Four kilometres from Ideles turn left at the sign for Tazrouk and Tahifet. Within 5km the piste begins to climb steeply. After 25km, you descend into the Oued Tassakimt and ride along its sandy course for a while before riding up the other side of the valley. After 46km you arrive at the junction for the piste to Tazrouk, marked by a giant concrete block. Tazrouk is another idyllic Tuareg mountain village which is used to receiving lost tourists heading for Tahifet. Fifty five kilometres south of the village is the spot where Colonel Flatters' Transsaharien railroad reconnaissance expedition was cut down by a Tuareg ambush in 1881. The massacre had the same effect on French national pride and resolve as had Custer's defeat for the Americans at the Little Big Horn, five years earlier. The story of the Flatters expeditions and other French Imperial follies in the Sahara are compellingly told in Douglas Porch's *Conquest of the Sahara* (see Books).

At the concrete block, keep right for the little-used piste between Tazrouk and Tahifet. Four kilometres from the block you will pass the alternative, sandy piste to Tazrouk, 20km away, following the course of the Oued Teberber. A little over-half way along this oued, near some fig trees at the base of the conical rock, Tihokin, are several engravings of long-vanished beasts and evidence of the hieroglyphic Libyan script on which the Tuareg tifinar text is based. Back an the main piste, you continue southwards, through a landscape of jumbled, granite boulders, and around the Col Azrou area the piste steepens and twists as it eventually descends to the Oued Azrou and Oued Tahifet.

From here it's a tiring ride, as you're trapped in sandy ruts along the narrow valleys that lead to Tahifet, 121km from Ideles. There is a bypass to the west (right) of town, otherwise ride through the village with its irrigated gardens, causing the usual commotion with the kids, and out across the sandy oued back on to the main piste. You are now back on a primary supply route that serves a string of villages from Tahifet to Tamanrasset: In Dalag, (keep right at 140km) and Tarhaouaout (keep right at 155km). Tarhaouaout (they love their 't's and vowels around here) is the site of the original French administrative centre in the Hoggar, then called Fort Motlinsky, built by General Laperrine in 1910.

It was Henri Laperrine who revolutionised France's attempt to con-

PISTES IN THE
HOGGAR (H)
MOUNTAINS

H1 TAM - ASSEKREM - TAM LOOP   180 km
H2 IDELES - HIRAFOK - IN AMGUEL   125 km
H3 IDELES - TAHIFET - TAM   250 km

© 1991
P. CORBETT

trol the Sahara by creating the independently mobile camel corps, *Les Saharians*. By adopting the ways of the desert nomad, this mixture of adept French NCOs and co-operative Chaamba nomads (conveniently, sworn enemies of the Tuareg) helped the French to subdue the warlike Tuareg at the Battle of Tit, near Tamanrasset, in 1902.

Back on the piste, a couple of kilometres after the turn south for Tarhaoaout, is a track leading northwest for 6km to the waterfall of

A.Sutton

Tamekrest. Don't count on a scene from a menthol cigarette advertisement. The main piste continues westwards again, descending into the Oued Tifougueguine, past the foot of Mount Debnat. Vegetation and trees proliferate as you churn through the sandy ruts or rattle over the corrugations to the village of Talan-n-Teidat. From here, you can see the back of the table mountain, Hadriane, which you will recognise from the campsite in Tamanrasset. Soon after the village you come across the sealed road, marked by a large concrete block Turn right for Tamanrasset, 7km to the north. If you've had a hard time, you may wish to kiss the tarmac at this point.

ROUTE I: REGGANE – GAO

Distance. 1365km – 853 miles.

Piste description. From Reggane to Bordj is featureless flat reg with occasional soft patches. From Tessalit the piste is rougher, corrugated while further south it's very sandy.

Fuel. Available at Reggane, Bordj Moktar, Tessalit (unofficially) and at Gao.

Water. Available at Reggane, then none till Bordj Moktar. From Tessalit southwards, you can get water from the village wells along the piste.

Maps. Recommended: IGN l:lm sheets NF31, NE31, Michelin 953. Useful: NG31.

Route description

This is one of the longest main routes in the entire Sahara, over 1300km of piste, totally desolate in its northern half and increasingly sandy towards the Niger river. Although route-finding is straightforward, it is much safer to ride in the company of other vehicles. The piste is marked all the way to Bordj Moktar, with solar beacons every 2km. They're supposed to flash by night and recharge by day, but most of them don't work or have been vandalised.

The piste immediately out of Reggane is corrugated and becomes sandy for the first 50km. After this, the ground firms up and the riding is smooth and easy. Two hundred kilometres from Reggane there is an old emergency water tank that has not been replenished in years. Fifty kilometres later is the long-abandoned Poste Weygand (also known as 'Balise 250' indicating the distance from Reggane). There is nothing here but some delapidated metal sheds and a piste leading to the old fort of Ouallen, 70km to the east. This was one of the French nuclear testing sites in the Sahara (another was near In Ecker) during the 1950's, before they moved on to the Pacific atolls. Three hundred and sixty kilometres from Reggane, an area of soft sand and dunes welcomes you to the tropics, as you cross 23.30° N; the Tropic of Cancer. After 400km you come across the second empty emergency water tank, once spaced every 200km across the Tanezrouft. Five hundred and fifteen kilometres from Reggane is the old navigation beacon and abandoned buildings of Bidon V or, 'oil drum number five', a marker left in 1920 by the first cars (Citroëns) to cross the Sahara. Bidon V grew to become an important airstrip and way-station in de Saint Exupery's time (see *Wind, Sand and Stars* in Books), but has now degenerated into an historic pile of scrap metal. South of Bidon V you cross the all-but-fizzled-out Oued Tamanrasset, another area of soft sand, with some vegetation and dunes. Bordj Moktar should appear as 640km (400 miles) clicks onto your odometer.

Fill up or wait for fuel, then check-out with the Police and Customs. The next stretch to Gao is slightly longer and more demanding. Leave to the southwest and at the junction, 32km from Bordj, turn south for Mali. Keeping straight on leads to Timiaouine in Algeria and a piste back

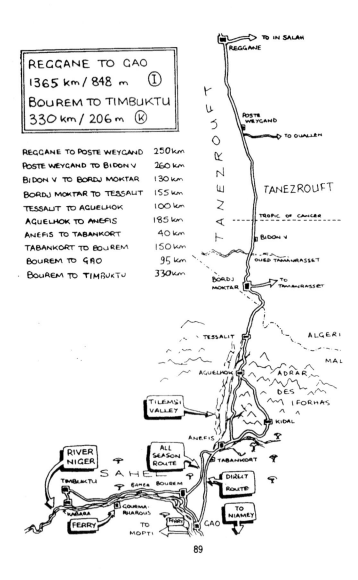

REGGANE TO GAO
1365 km / 848 m   (I)
BOUREM TO TIMBUKTU
330 km / 206 m   (K)

REGGANE TO POSTE WEYGAND	250 km
POSTE WEYGAND TO BIDON V	260 km
BIDON V TO BORDJ MOKTAR	130 km
BORDJ MOKTAR TO TESSALIT	155 km
TESSALIT TO AGUELHOK	100 km
AGUELHOK TO ANEFIS	185 km
ANEFIS TO TABANKORT	40 km
TABANKORT TO BOUREM	150 km
BOUREM TO GAO	95 km
BOUREM TO TIMBUKTU	330 km

89

to Tamanrasset (see route F). There are no more solar beacons in Mali but the track is clear. The piste deviates through a oued about 100km from Bordj. It is possible to become disorientated in this area, make sure you keep right to avoid a sensitive military zone hereabouts. Tessalit is set among rocky hills, 155km from Bordj. Go straight to the Police and Customs first, and leave your beer in the cafe for later. Once your business is done you may wish to rest in some of the campements that have sprung up south of the town, although whether they have survived the Tuareg siege of this area in recent times will only be clear when this route re-opens. You can buy fuel at Tessalit from entrepreneurs at a fair price. You will also be offered a guide to take you south, along the Oued Tilemsi, which runs parallel to the main route, a little to the west. It's the reputed home of gazelles and other wildlife, and guiding you is the only way a Tessalitian can get a lift south and be paid for it!

A hundred kilometres from Tessalit (250km from Bordj) is the village of Aguelhok, with water, a police checkpoint and a piste to the forbidden military zone at Kidal, in the Adrar des Iforhas highlands which is closed to tourists. Three hundred and fifty kilometres from Bordj is a 10km section of grassy sand hummocks known as the Markouba Sands which have finished off many a moribund Peugeot 504. Even on a bike, it can be an exhausting ride that has to be tackled with some assertiveness, especially as you will now be more aware of the warmer temperatures. It's easier to cross the Sands (and any other area of soft sand, for that matter) early in the morning, when any nighttime condensation has bound the surface grains together just enough to make a difference to traction. The air temperature is also cooler for a hard-working engine.

After 420km you pass the main piste to Kidal (see above) and 15km later you'll ride through the poor, windblown village of Anefis, which has a well and a police control post. If no one challenges you, don't bother stopping to report. You have now converged with the watercourse of the Tilemsi and at Tabankort, 475km from Bordj, you head west along the more commonly used piste to Bourem and Gao. By continuing south of Tabankort you follow the alternative piste along the Tilemsi directly to Gao. There are more 'Markouba' type obstacles and it can be impassable following rain. However, even the next 100km of the main route to Bourem are very sandy at times, with dunes right across the piste. It is hard work on a fully loaded bike, but not impossible. The village of Bourem and the Niger river are 565km from Bordj Mocktar. The riverside market, brimming with exotic produce, spices and fish may be your first taste of West Africa's colour and vitality. Brace yourself for the pestering attentions of the kids; at Gao and Timbuktu they're even worse. The police may want to check you out, depending on their mood.

Gao is another 95km south, along the bank of the river via the village of Tondibi. Check-in With the police on arrival. Seven kilometres south of Gao is a motor ferry across the Niger. From the opposite bank a tarmac road leads to Mopti and the capital, Bamako. A very sandy piste continues south from the ferry along the river to Asongo and the Niger frontier at Labezanga.

ROUTE J: TAMANRASSET - ARLIT

Distance. 655km – 409 miles.

Piste conditions. The tarmac ends some 200km south of Tamanrasset. Diverse tracks with corrugations and some sandy sections head south to Laouni, where the various pistes converge and corrugate down to In Guezzam. Apart from the odd soft patch towards Assamaka, the section from here to Arlit is mostly firm and fast.

Fuel. Available at Tam, In Guezzam and Arlit. Your fuel range must well exceed the 400km to In Guezzam.

Water. As above.

Maps. Recommended: IGN I:Im sheet NF31.

Route description

Recent reports suggest that the tarmac road now stretches half-way to the Algerian frontier at In Guezzam, which makes this long and featureless section easier to travel with every passing year.

Ride down to the tarmac's end, about 200km from Tamanrasset. From this point there are many tracks and occasional *balises* (marked I GZ and a distance in km) which converge around the dunes at the fort of Laouni, about 100km from the end of the tarmac. With dunes to the east and the distant escarpment of Gara-Ekar to the west, the piste becomes widely corrugated as it funnels through the hills towards In Guezzam. There is fuel and a cafe (with a well) at In Guezzam. It's your last chance to get rid of your dinars which can't be taken out of the country. Note that returning to Tamanrasset is officially forbidden - you can't come to In Guezzam just for the ride. The customs post will expect all your papers to be in order before they let you go. The *feche-feche* (fine powdery sand) on the way to Assamaka, 25km from In Guezzam, is nowhere near as bad as the Sahara Handbook makes out. At Assamaka, there's a cafe, a tree and a Police and Customs post, although a refugee camp may have sprung up here too, by now. From Assamaka head southeast into a flat, featureless void, punctuated by drums at 2km intervals. South of here, Alan Cooper and some of his party perished in their Morris Traveller in 1955 (see *Trek* in Books). Once at Arlit, 80km from Assamaka, the cultural divide on the south side of the Sahara will be evidently clear and worthy of celebration.

ROUTE K: BOUREM – TIMBUKTU

Distance. 330 km – 206 miles.

Piste conditions. Sandy ruts most of the way. This piste is physically demanding on a loaded bike. A couple of miles south of Timbuktu, join the tarmac road that leads to the town.

Fuel. Available at Gao (95km south of Bourem) and Timbuktu (at a price!).

Water. Plenty of it in the Niger river and in Timbuktu (you may have to pay a small fee).

Maps. Useful IGN 1:1m sheet NE31, Michelin 953.

Route description

The piste is clear all the way to Timbuktu, technically at its easiest when following the banks or cracked muddy inlets of the river. If you do become disorientated, you can be certain that the river is somewhere to your left (south). Otherwise it is very sandy, with no alternative to the twin-rutted track that winds over dunes, with light, thorny vegetation to either side. On a loaded road bike it might prove to be impossible (as it will be for ordinary cars), but then Timbuktu hasn't become a metaphor for 'the ends of the earth' for nothing.

Two kilometres north of Bourem the piste leads westwards into the low dunes. Keep going for 140km until you get to the village of Bamba, by the river. A tiny cafe in a shack might offer you welcome shade and refreshment. After Bamba, the piste gets even sandier but 180km from Bourem at Chargo there's a barge that can take you over the river to Gourma-Rharous,

TIMBUKTU

"Is that it?" was Bob Geldof's lacklustre impression of the fabled Golden City where "camel meets canoe". Today Timbuktu isn't much to look at. Its original Djingguerber mosque is just another mud-brick and stick mosque, of the sort commonly found in the Sahel. The great mosque was built in the 14th century to celebrate the Mali Empire's liberation of Timbuktu from extortionate Tuareg control, the mosque's original golden roof consolidating the city's reputation for fabulous wealth. These riches were engendered by the city's strategic position, a port from which salt, gold and slaves crossed the Sahara to the Maghreb and Europe. Indeed, most of medieval Europe's gold originated from West Africa, still mined today in southwest Mali. When the liberating Emperor Mansa Musa passed through Cairo on his pilgrimage to Mecca, he gave out so many gold coins (up to a ton and a half) that the price of the precious metal crashed locally for years. As the wealth and stability of Timbuktu grew, it became established as a seat of legal and religious study, accommodating up to 25,000 students during the 16th century, the city's most prosperous period.

During this time, the Tuaregs again began menacing the city (nothings changed in 500 years...), demanding tribute from the caravans coming and going to the city. Later, under the protection of the Songhai Empire, Timbuktu was freed from Tuareg influence and prospered to a degree which today is difficult to comprehend. Other cities, like the Songhai capital, Gao and Oualata (in present day Mauritania) has similar reputations, thriving as centres of trade, culture and learning. Word of the Songhai riches spread north with the caravans to Morocco and Europe, and in 1591 the Sultan of Marrakesh's army marched across the Sahara, sacking the Songhai cities and plundering their fabulous wealth. The once great Empire crumbled almost overnight, and from that date the city fell into a dark age of paganism and progressive decline.

However, over the intervening years the legend of the Golden City south of the Great Desert seeped into the imaginations of the Europeans, who were themselves discovering and exploiting the new found riches of the Orient. By the early 19th century, the learned societies of Britain and France offered fantastic financial rewards to the first to return with corroborative reports of 'Timbuktu'. The Scot, Gordon Laing was the first of the explorers to get there in 1826, travelling across the Sahara from Tripoli, while the Frenchman, Rene Caille, got there two years later. Dressed as a local, Caille managed to return to France alive, escaping Laing's murderous fate just north of the city. The Americans could also claim that the shipwrecked sailor, Robert Adams, beat them both by seventeen years, when he was taken to Timbuktu, but being a slave rather than a competitive explorer on a lucrative quest, history has counted him out.

Today the houses which Laing, Caille, and the notable German scholar Heinrich Barth stayed in, are marked with plaques for the benefit of visiting tourists. By the time the 19th century explorers had exploded the myth of Timbuktu, the city was already a shadow of its former self. Five hundred years ago up to 100,000 people lived here in varied splendour. These days less than 5000 descendants of the merchants and conquerors struggle to survive against the ever-encroaching desert which bears down on the town. Most western visitors don't mind what the place looks like as long as they can say they've been there, but the unremitting hassle from the pathologically gregarious local children has caused some sensitive tourists to flee the city in tears! Lodging here is an expensive business. Young spies inform the campsite manager whether any *toubabs* have managed to secure hospitality from a local, where they are soon exposed and sent to the campsite, hotel or asked to leave. To be frank, Timbuktu has little to offer the curious visitor other than its genuine isolation and fascinating history.

if you've had enough. From Gourma, a 150km piste leads to the tarmac road just north of Gossi. Thierry Sabine, founder and organiser of the Paris-Dakar Rally, died near Gourma-Rharous during the 1986 event. While searching for stragglers during a sandstorm, his helicopter crashed, killing all occupants. The rally had taken a certain pride in becoming increasingly extreme with each passing year and many more were to lose their lives in the '86 Rally. Sabine's ashes were scattered across the Ténéré Desert, where he nearly died while lost during one of the early Abidjan–Nice Rallies.

The sand lets up a bit after Chargo, and after 32km you reach a short section of tarmac road which leads up to the legendary city of Timbuktu.

USEFUL ADDRESSES

Embassies

- **ALGERIA**. 6 Hyde Park Gate, London, SW7 1QQ. (☎0171/221 7800) Applications in person only.

- **CHAD**. The French Consulate (☎0171/235 8080) deals with visas for Chad, Like most consular offices, they are not very sympathetic to telephone enquiries. Allow several weeks for the visa to be issued.

- **LIBYA**. Worldwide Visas (see below) will attempt to obtain a visa for you. Libya requires a translation of your passport details into Arabic.

- **MALI** and **MAURITANIA**. Both at 89 rue de la Cherche-Midi, Paris 75006 Allow six weeks or apply in person; it will take one or two days. In Madrid the Mauritanian embassy is at

- **Worldwide Visas**. 9 Adelaide Street, London WC2N 4HZ. (direct line ☎0171/379 0419; recorded information ☎0891 616466). Does the queuing up and waiting for you, which can be useful if you don't live in London, where most of the consular offices are located. A Mali visa (from Paris) costs £95 including all courier fees and takes a fortnight. Any visa acquired in London costs from £25 plus the cost of the visa.

Equipment Suppliers & Bike Preparation

- **Alf Hagon**. 7–9 Fowler Rd, Hainault, Essex. Shock absorbers, security bolts and heavy duty spokes plus wheelbuilding with Akront rims.

- **Bernd Tesch Globetrott-Zentrale**. Karlsgraben 69, D–52064 Aachen-Centrum, Germany (☎00 49241/33636; Fax 00 49241/39494). Round the world bike enthusiast with a catalogue full of gear including big tanks, alloy cases and racks for commonly used desert bikes, especially BMWs.

- **Bracken M.W**. 330 St. James Road. London, SE1 (☎0171/231 9438). BMW desert/overland preparation and advice plus new and used spares. Owner has experience on BMs and Africa Twins in North African rallies.

- **Cotswold Camping**. 42-46 Uxbridge Rd, London W12 8NP (☎0181/743 2976) and branches in Cirencester, Southampton, Reading, Manchester and Betws-y-Çoed. Outdoor shops with enthusiastic staff and a wide range of gear including all of the water filters recommended in this book. Free mail order catalogue.

- **Därrs Travel Shop**. Theresienstrasse 66, 8000, Munich 2, Germany. (☎00 49 89 2/82032). Stanfords and Cotsworld and all in one place. Includes bike luggage systems. Also a drool-worthy catalogue for £1.

- **Moto-Ward**. 117 Brighton Road, Surbiton, Surrey KT6 SNJ. (☎0181/399 0630). Off-road bike shop that sells, or can order, Acerbis plastic fuel tanks, etc.

- **M&P Accessories**. Unit 3 Castell Close, Swansea Enterprise Park, Llansamlet, Swansea, SA7 1XX (☎01792/775566; Fax 01792/781452). Huge mail order parts and accessory supplier. Of interest to desert bikers are Riky trail bike products which include frame stiffeners/bag supports, as well as racks and other, more cosmetic, add ons.

- **Nomad Travel Shop**. 3-4 Wellington Terrace, Turnpike Lane, London N8 0PX (☎0181/889 7014). Specialises in equipment for the tropics with a useful travel pharmacy offering expert travel health advice as well as pre-packed first aid kits.

- **Survival Aids**. Morland, Penrith, Cumbria, CA10 3AZ (☎01931/714444). Eight shops in England and Scotland. Outdoor and camping equipment, including compact water purifiers. Winter and summer catalogues available.

- **Telesonic Marine**. 60-64 Brunswick Centre, Marchmont St, London, WC1N 8AE (☎0171/837 4106). Sailing equipment which includes a good range of hand held GPS receivers at substantially discounted prices. Ask for their catalogue.

Insurance & Travel

- **Campbell Irvine Insurance**. 46 Earls Court Road, London W8 6EJ (☎0171/937 9903). Travel medical and Carnet insurance service.

- **Southern Ferries**. 179 Piccadilly, London W1V 9DB (☎0171/491 4968). SNCM brochure available for ferry routes from southern Europe to North Africa. At the same address are SNCF whose Motorail service (☎0171/409 3518) can deliver you and your bike from Paris to Marseille overnight from £30 return. A second-class passenger fare is a few pounds less, off-peak, well worth considering in winter (☎0171/409 3518). In Marseille, the head office of SNCM is at 61, boulevard des Dames, Marseilles, 13002.

- **Dust Trails**. 187 Staines Rd, Laleham, Staines, Middx, TW18 2SD (☎01784/461542 or ☎01985/841184). Only UK-based adventure bike tour company run by two experienced overland bikers. At present they offer two week escorted trips through the Moroccan Atlas and Sahara in Spring and autumn for around £1250 but trips to southern Tunisia and longer treks are in the pipeline. Dust Trails may also be able to supply you with specialist gear (big tanks, Michelin Desert tyres, etc) for your trip.

- **Agence Temet Voyages**. B.P. 178 Agadez, Niger (☎440051). Paris office at 71 rue des Nouettes, 75015, Paris (☎00 33 48 28 Z0 49). Organisers of tours in the Ténéré Desert and Aïr mountains. May not be around any more following recent events in the central Sahara

- **Wüstenfahrer Reise gmbh**. Friedenstrasse 26, 8012 Ottobrunn. (☎/Fax 004989/609 7707). German company specialising in adventurous motorbike touring in the Sahara run by Thomas Trossmann, an expert in this field (see Books).

Book Shops & Further Information

- **Travellers' Bookshop** 25 Cecil Court, London WC2N 4EZ (☎0171/836 9132; Fax 0171/379 4928. Publishers of this book and specialist travel book shop which includes antiquerian and current-edition secondhand guides, a travellers notice board and tea and coffee making facilities.

- **Daunts** 83 Marylebone High St, London W1 3DE (☎0171/224 2295). London's best browsing travel bookshop with heaps of room and rarely crowded. Secondhand and cooking books are mixed in with the usual regional travel guides. Well worth a visit.

- **Stanfords Map And Travel Bookshop** 12-14 Long Acre, London, WC2E 9LP. (☎0171/836 1321). French IGN and American DMA maps of the Sahara, as well as travel literature and guide books.

- **Travel Bookshop** 13 Blenheim Crescent, London W11 3EE (☎0171/229 5260). Cosy book shop with many secondhand and foreign travel guidebooks. Has a good Africa section.

- **Royal Geographical Society** 1 Kensington Gore, London, SW7 2AR. Includes Expedition Advisory Centre (EAC; ☎0171/581 2057), as well as access to Map Room and old expedition reports for nonmembers.

- **Institut Geographique National** map centre, 107 rue de la boetie, Paris, 75008. Full range of IGN maps and also travel books.

AGAINST THE GRAINS: TRUE STORIES FROM THE SAHARA

Now you've read about the practicalities of preparing for a desert trip on your bike and you've got a rough idea what it's all about, sit back while the welds cool on your home-made rack and read some true tales of desert biking.

DESERT STORM
by Si Melber

It is five o'clock in the morning and I am lying in a dusty hotel room in downtown Ghardaia in the north of Algeria, blinking in the darkness. From one of the town's many minarets the wailing begins again, calling the faithful to prayer with one word sung over and over. 'Alaaaaaah'. Suddenly there is another voice from another minaret, this time higher and slightly more off-pitch, but the tune is similar, and the one and only lyric repeated monotonously. 'Alaaaaaah'.

I slump back down in my bed and think about the previous four weeks. My first taste of the world's largest desert, with its huge sand seas and dunes that stretch uninterrupted as far as the eye can see. The rocky plateaux that characterise much of the central Sahara, the towering beauty of the Hoggar mountains, and how I came to be nursing a broken rib.

You could fit the whole of Australia into the Sahara and still have some left over. It stretches for three-and-a-half-million square miles through more than a dozen North African countries and you cannot begin to comprehend its size simply by looking at a map. It is simply vast.

It's the sheer scale of the desert, along with the remoteness of much of it, that has drawn overlanders here like a magnet. At its heart, in the south of Algeria, lies the town of Tamanrasset, the overlanders' equivalent of Mecca, and my destination aboard Kawasaki's new KLX650.

I had been invited to North Africa by *Dust Trails,* a new overland company catering for people who wanted to ride the Sahara with the security of a four-wheel-drive back-up truck. I met up with the nine other British riders at the dockside in Genoa, northern Italy, and 25 hours later I was at the customs in Tunis, showing my passport for the ninth time and refusing to pay a bribe – my first taste of African bureaucracy. Finally, they impounded the truck overnight, declining to release it the following morning until a substantial amount of wedge had been handed over, along with a large can of corned beef.

Tunisia is a beautiful country, typically Mediterranean and reminiscent of Turkey or Greece. Fruit stalls line the road and a glass of fresh-ly-squeezed juice costs only a few pence. The roads themselves are pol-ished to a mirror finish and covered in a thin layer of dust, which makes riding quite hazardous, especially when swerving to avoid the myriad ani-mals that seem to inhabit them. Chickens, goats, dogs, sheep and a herd of cows on a blind bend kept us constantly on our toes, while prepos-terously overloaded pick-up trucks performed gung-ho overtaking manoeuvres past wheezing old mopeds. At one stage our support truck was forced into a ditch by an oncoming lorry which refused to move from its death or glory position straddling the central white line. Through it all the Kawasaki thundered on over glacier-smooth roads past dusty villages lined with waving children.

Stopping briefly to buy some fruit in the town of Kairouan, the bikes were immediately surrounded by a crowd of youngsters jostling to secure a better look. Everywhere we went the bikes drew admiring glances: toothless old men would smile and then gesture with their right hands as if opening a fictitious throttle, and children would gather around and chatter.

The road that crosses the Chott El Djerid salt flats is perfectly straight for almost sixty miles, but it's possible to ride across the flats themselves, which vary in texture from a hard white crust to sticky mud and occasional patches of water. Slithering our way through the ooze on trail tyres was memorable, but left the bikes caked in a salty residue that resisted all attempts at cleaning. The occasional abandoned vehicle was a grim reminder that parts of the flats were impassable and best avoid-ed. Soon after, we run into out first dust storm.

Sticking as close together as possible, we crawled along in the chok-ing dust with our headlights on. At times visibility was reduced to just 15 feet by the sand-laden wind which scoured our unprotected skin. Just as suddenly as it arrived, the darkness seemed to lift and the storm passed over. Approaching the frontier with Algeria at dusk we stopped just short to spend the night in a palm grove among the sand dunes and scorpions.

The following day's border crossings took us a further eight hours and relieved us of two bottles of Jack Daniels, numerous cigarettes and a box of King Edward cigars. But at last we were in Algeria and the start of the desert proper. The road to Touggourt was our first real taste of the sand that was to come, passing through the northern flank of the Grand Erg Oriental. Huge dunes lined both sides of the road and spilled across it, making fast progress difficult. It is a full time job for the Algerian authorities to keep roads like this clear, as the stack of partially buried earthmovers bears testament. The shifting sands pay no attention to highways driven through their midst and judging by the amount of sand on the road it won't be long before this stretch of tarmac disappears completely.

Searching for a place to spend the night we happened across a tiny village where we were made welcome, and entertained on traditional cous-cous and hot mint tea (not to mention half a dozen massive spliffs). At midnight we joined a wedding celebration before retiring bleary-eyed to sleep in one of the village huts. The following morning a local hot spring provided our first bath since leaving Italy, and bread, coffee and fried camel was the next best thing to a full English breakfast. The village children had risen early in anticipation of our leaving, and the morning was spent giving them rides around the village on the back of the bikes. Leaving them T-shirts and baseball caps in return for their hospitality, we headed for Hassi-Messaoud and a fuel stop to fill up our jerricans in preparation for the next leg of our journey.

The road out of Hassi Messaoud heads due south for more than 250 miles through the heart of the Grand Erg Oriental, and most of the bikes took the opportunity to nail it across the sand, sending up huge plumes of dust in their trails. But the unpredictability of the terrain is legend, smooth hard sand can give way to bumps and hollows that fill with dust disguising their presence, and can have you off the bike in seconds.

My first endo came after a few hours of this sort of riding, when hammering along at about 50mph I came across a patch of bumpy ground I hadn't spotted. Hitting a jump at speed I landed badly and before I could correct it found myself on a couple of big rocks, the bike bucked up into the air and spat me off straight over the handlebars. As I stood up and dusted myself down there was the sound of hissing air and I looked down to find the front tyre flatter than a one-legged hedgehog in a road crossing race.

Whoever coined the phrase 'we learn from our mistakes' was either a smug bastard or a damned liar because within an hour I had done it all again only this time more painfully (breaking my rib in the process) and all the time under the watchful eye of the video camera (it still hurts to see it played back). Still, after I had managed to get my breath back I staggered back to where I had taken off and counted out a very painful 11 metres to the point of contact with the ground – ouch.

The Kawasaki had faired better than me, and apart from bends in the handlebars and rear brake lever had survived unscathed. More worrying, however, was that the rear suspension had begun to bottom out over medium-sized bumps and with the preload wound up full there was no more adjustment left. What's more, it was clear that under full compression the rear tyre was making contact with the bottom of the mudguard because of insufficient clearance. I wondered what it was going to be like with a set of knobblies fitted which were even taller. In the end I didn't have to wait long to find out.

Riding alongside the truck the following day, a series of small bumps in quick succession hammered the wheel into the mudguard five or six times, the last time ripping out the inner guard and exposing the wiring loom and airbox to a severe beating. Roadside repairs with gaff tape and cable ties got it mobile again, but the damage had been done. I decided it was time for me to spend the day aboard the truck, fixing the bike and giving me a chance to shoot some photos. By the end of the morning the bike had been repaired with some truck inner tube taped in place of the missing mudguard. This was a temporary fix but would have to do for the next 1000 miles.

The rest of the day was spent lying on the rood of the truck watching the warm North African skies go by. Were it not for the problem with the bike I would have been completely contented laying there that day feeling the warm breeze wash over me and soaking up the scenery. By the time we arrived in Hassi Bel Guebbour (Hassi Bugger all) the rest of the bikes had installed themselves in the one and only cafe and were sitting on the veranda eating dates and cheese sandwiches. Contentment all round I think. That evening we camped at the foot of an escarpment and climbed up to survey the scene as darkness fell. Except for our campfire flickering the distance, there was nothing else to see for miles in any direction – the sense of isolation was difficult to comprehend.

A puncture on one of the bikes and half-an-hour spent digging the truck out of soft sand delayed our start the following morning as we followed the road that led along the edge of the Tinrhert plateau. To the south of us lay a 1000-foot drop and a spectacular view over the Erg Issaouane, but by the side of the road there was increasingly more evidence of the oil exploration that scars this part of the Sahara. Mammoth trucks had churned up the desert floor and stockpiles of drill casings awaiting use had turned this stretch into one large building site.

The drop down through the Grand Falaise from the Tinrhert plateau was as spectacular as it was easy: the roads were good, the temperature was rising, and we were heading for more dunes. So far, apart from minor spills and get-offs we had avoided any major endos. Within 50 miles that clean record had come to an abrupt end.

Desert dunes are quite unlike the sort of thing you find on your local beach. Lacking any vegetation to bind them or any water to level them out, they are generated entirely by the prevailing wind. Though seemingly random, they generally follow a pattern and structure that is as reliable as the rising sun. The leeward slope is the shallower, and can be firm enough to support a bike, peaking in a precise knife-edged ridge beyond which the sand drops away steeply and loosely.

It was while crossing one edge of the Erg Issaouane dunes that one of the party suffered the only serious accident of the entire trip. Cresting a dune without stopping on the top, he dropped 30 feet off the downwind side, badly dislocating his shoulder and terminating the front end of his Yamaha XT600 in the process. Seeing one of our number lying unconscious at the bottom of a dune pinned down by his bike served as a grim reminder of how dangerous dune riding can be if you lose concentration even for a second. The hospital in nearby Illizi was only three uncomfortable hours away by truck, but for him the trip was over before the serious off-roading had begun.

Illizi marks the end of the tarmac road from the north. Between it and Tamanrasset there is nothing but fabulous scenery and desolation for 500 miles. Leaving the confines of the campsite the corrugations mark the beginning of the off-road section and the climb up onto the Fadnoun plateau – 150 miles of bare rock littered with sharp-edged sandstone boulders. Picking our way through the rock-strewn track required enormous levels of concentration and much of the going was tackled in second gear.

After 30 miles the KLX's front tyre punctured again, many of the other bikes suffering a similar fate. A few miles later, one of the Super Ténéré riders fell off trying to avoid a flying rock, destroying the bike's fairing in the process. As the light began to fade the going became even more hazardous, and when we finally pulled over to camp we had travelled just 60 miles in six hours.

Next day, with tyre pressures running at 35psi to resist further punctures, we bounced and skipped our way across the remainder of the plateau through ravines and deep gorges until at last descending an escarpment into the sand of the Tassili N'Ajjer. Racing across the soft sand with the truck and the other bikes thundering along under clear blue skies was an incredible feeling. There is no track, just a vast expanse of sand as far as you can see. It's a weird sensation being able to ride a full 360-degrees in any direction without obstruction, and the KLX was in its element storming along in top gear.

A change to knobbly tyres that evening helped the bike in the soft sand next day, as it writhed and weaved at speed, fighting to find direction. The terrain was mostly flat marked piste with the occasional hollow to catch the unwary. The constant backdrop of mountains at times forced us into the narrow gorges which wound between them, opening out again to reveal vast dusty plains scattered with thorn trees.

Continuing our south-westerly route, the piste passed Fort Serenout, a long-abandoned French Foreign Legion fort in the shadow of an extinct volcano. It is the only man-made landmark for hundreds of miles and makes you wonder what exactly they were guarding. For another 120 miles the sandy going was fast and furious but in the background the fabulous Hoggar mountains that marked the end of our journey loomed ever nearer. All the while colossal granite spires rose up around us from the desert floor, the remains of long-extinct volcanoes worn away by the elements to reveal their rocky cores.

The little town of Ideles lies at an altitude of 4600 feet and is remarkable for nothing except its solar powered street-lighting illuminating a motley collection of ramshackle old houses. It was our resting place for the assault on the Hoggar mountains and our next destination, the remote hermitage of Assekrem. The track to Assekrem climbs steadily along a winding path littered with rocks and wash-outs, crossing the Tropic of Cancer as it does so. At best the going is difficult, but the scenery more than makes up for it. All around, trachyte basoliths rise up from a granite plain seemingly piercing the clear blue sky with their jagged peaks.

Around every corner a vista opens up − each view better than the last, each climb steeper than the one before. At this altitude the KLX's lack of real bottom end power was beginning to tell. Climbing slopes required a huge handful of throttle which only resulted in unsticking the back end. Not at all what you need given the daunting drops that marked the edge of the track.

The final ascent up to Assekrem is a seemingly endless procession of loose-surface hairpins leading up to a small but welcoming hostel perched at 6500 feet on the side of a mountain. Inside, a roaring log fire greeted us, and a bowl of cous-cous and strong dark coffee fortified us for the hard night ahead − because of the altitude, temperatures regularly drop below freezing.

The following morning we rose before dawn and climbed the steep path that leads up to the hermitage where two monks sat praying in a tiny chapel. Standing in the chill morning air, we watched in stunned silence as the first rays of sunshine illuminated the shadowy Hoggar mountains. Assekrem is without doubt one of the most remarkable places anywhere in the world, and for me the highlight of the whole trip.

The final leg to Tamanrasset and our first shower in eight days meant once again picking our route through the rocky path that passes for the road here. Within a mile the KLX had punctured and half a mile later it happened again after picking up a huge thorn. As I sat by the side of the road repairing the bike, a huge eagle swooped gracefully overhead coming to rest on a nearby crag and sat watching me struggle. Not wishing to become eagle fodder I hastily repaired the tyre and pressed on down the track.

Tamanrasset was a bustling market town full of beaten up Land Rovers and ancient Peugeot taxis. Here at last I could buy fresh food and clean out the weeks of debris that had accumulated in the bottom of my boots. Refreshingly clean and smelling of Wash & Go, I set about sniffing out the nearest local hostelry that could provide me with a chilled bottle or two of Algeria's finest. From here on it was north all the way.

(A version of the above feature originally appeared in the May, 1993 edition of *Motorcycle International* magazine. Si Melber is the editor of *Trail Bike* magazine)

DESERT DEBUT

I left Algeria's southernmost town, Tamanrasset, with loaded jerricans and visa stamped, and headed south towards In Guezzam, on the border with Niger. Fifty lovely, smooth, bend-swinging kilometres of new tarmac winding through rocky hills lasted about 45 minutes out of Tam. Then a small sign read "*Route barée*". The piste, which I and my ridiculously overloaded XT500 had been fearing for days, was upon us.

Seven hundred kilometres and maybe two or three days riding further south, some semblance of road would resume near Arlit in Niger. Between these points lay a barren wilderness of sand and rocky plains, punctuated half way by the In Guezzam/ Assamaka frontier posts, which you couldn't afford to miss. I rode past the Algerian road crews, still building the road that will eventually seal the Sahara with tar from the Mediterranean to the Gulf of Guinea.

On to the piste, feet dabbing, struggling but unable to attain momentum in soft sand ruts, I fell off almost immediately. "It'll take me a week at this rate. It must get better." And at times it did, as my confidence grew and I managed a nervous third gear. The route opened up into the enormous Oued Tin Amzi, a dried-up river bed riddled with corrugations that tried to thrash bike and spine into early graves; but I knew that worse was yet to come. The guidebook had warned of a vast sea of *feche-feche* surrounding In Guezzam – fine, soft and deep sand capped by a meringue-like crust but much less tasty.

Occasionally, an oil drum or marker post – called *balises* – indicated that I was still on the right track, but eventually they, and the reassuring *oued* petered out into open country. Hundreds of ruts wound generally southwards, as each passing vehicle had strived to avoid corrugations and soft patches. Each unavoidable patch of *feche-feche*, sometimes distinguishable from surrounding terrain by being slightly lighter in colour, made the engine moan with effort as the tyres sunk in. It was WFO at all costs, until I was trapped in first gear and had to jump off and run alongside, desperately trying to maintain momentum.

Real danger was presented by the occasional and unpredictable, foot-high ledges cut by rare floods or late summer sandstorms. The paradox of riding fast enough to overcome soft sand yet slow enough to stop in time for the ledges sapped my concentration and was nervously exhausting. Anyway, the fact that I'd long since smashed the XT's front brake lever off in a first day crash meant that the quickest way to stop was falling off.

After hours of this stuff, I learned a guarded style, occasionally unsettled by surprise obstacles. Towards mid-afternoon I reached a firm sand plain and rejoiced in the relative relaxation of sweeping past the rougher bits at 60mph in approximately southward curves. Reaching back to check that my food and jerricans were still attached to the bike after hitting some unexpected ripples, I saw a lonely sign announcing "In Guezzam 285km". I had been travelling slower than hoped and doubted reaching the abandoned fort at Laouni by nightfall.

Continuing onward, I spotted another *balise* with relief. I stopped and leant the bike against it to take some photographs. Turning my back on an infinity of sand and rubble, I noticed a damp patch under the bike and a smell of petrol in the air. An optimistic prayer that it was just a sticky float quickly degenerated into panic as I realised that my specially made alloy five-gallon tank had cracked and was steadily leaking. I urgently rode on, looking for . . . I didn't know what.

'What' turned out to be a wrecked and abandoned BMW 2002, affording psychological shelter at least. I was still 200km from In Guezzam and there were only one-and-a-half hours of daylight left. Desperate to conserve precious fuel, I tore the luggage and seat off to inspect the damage before attempting to repair the cracked rear-bracket weld with Araldite. It didn't work. I decided to leave the second try to dry overnight, and tried to decide what to do. Would my reduced reserves of fuel last through more power-sapping *feche-feche* to Arlit? Would an already doubtful tank last over another 2000km of rough tracks until I reached the relative luxury of Ougadougou, capital of Upper Volta [Burkina Faso], which reputedly boasted a Yamaha dealer? Anyway, would my money run out before Abidjan? I spent the evening reading by candlelight in the scrap car shell, listening nervously to burrowing gerbils which *could* have been tarantulas or scorpions, and decided to return home. I'd seen the desert and wasn't very impressed – I accepted the defeat of an idea that I'd never really expected to succeed.

Next morning, the repair still hadn't worked, so I had another go with the last of the glue, and set off back towards Tamanrasset at about 10.30am, my shirt crammed between tank and frame to isolate it from further vibration. I'd scrawled a message on the car's side and had 20 litres of spare fuel in the jerrican, although the split tank was nearly empty. Luck would get me over the estimated 200km to the tarmaced road and civilization in, maybe, four hours.

Some hope. Almost straight away, I got into a scary pace, riding too fast and hitting all the bumps I sought o avoid. Panic rose, and a dangerous sense of urgency. I hit a sandwash ridge too quickly and knackered shocks ejected me over the 'bars. The tank and handlebars survived, but I soon had a couple more near misses – heartstopping tank slappers and broadsides. I felt that I was running for my life and didn't recognise any of the landmarks from the previous day. "It doesn't matter", I thought, "once I hit the big *oued*, it'll lead straight back to the new road." But, as I was about to find out, many *oueds* drain from the mighty Hoggar.

At 1.00pm I saw a sign claiming "Tamanrasset 135km" and pulled up for a fly-pestered rest. I could see the Hoggar mountains on the horizon and knew Tam was in the southwest corner of the massif. I found a *oued* and followed it with pathetic trust. Inexplicably, it turned west and then south after only a short distance. I tried a tributary creek, until it disappeared into sandstone rubble hills.

Struggling up the valley side, bashing sump plate and panniers on boulders, the over-loaded trail bike was exhausting to handle. From the ridge, I'd hoped to see the road, shining like a fresh black ribbon. But there was only another big dry river bed which similarly confounded me by turning south. I just tried heading north, looking for the firmest terrain among a lot of fine sand. Happily, I spotted an army jeep and some grazing animals. "Good, any minute now – the road", I thought. Paddling desperately in the powdery sand, I slithered in and out of bushes and thorn trees until the creek bed came to an end. It was *Shit Creek* and, as a horribly familiar weave from the back wheel announced a puncture, I realised I'd left my paddle in San Francisco.

Before extracting the buried thorn tips from the tyre and repairing it, I decided to climb the nearest big hill for a look around. At the top, someone had stuck a stick in the summit, probably a thousand years ago. I scanned the horizon, shading my brow like some classic explorer. No road. No Tamanrasset. No nothing. And then, what looked like a camp of camouflaged army tents caught my eye to the southwest, back down the main creek. "Well that's lucky, I'm saved", I grinned, my caution tempered by rampant optimism.

An hour later I'd fixed the puncture and set off, retracing my tracks down the *oued* and fifteen minutes later, I struck the road – nice, juicy, blacktop. Was it my road – how many roads are there out here and anyway, which way for Tamanrasset? I took a gamble to the right and was back in town in half an hour. I never found the army camp. It was probably a mirage offered by pitying *djenouns*, the spirits or genies of the desert.

(A version of the above feature titled 'Scott of the Sahara' originally appeared in the March, 1985 edition of *Which Bike* magazine and the *Which Bike Touring Guide – 1985*.

NAME THAT DUNE

Late morning in Arak, southern Algeria. I crouched against the shady wall outside the cafe. With a petrol pump, the well and the grass huts round the back, this constituted a pretty good place for a travellers' rest in this part of the Sahara.

My teeth scratched across a piece of bread that not twenty four hours ago had been warm and fresh. As I gnawed, I remembered the deservedly humiliating bollocking I'd received in this very spot last year for driving my anti-techno "Bénélé" (a CD200 mated to an AJS scrambler – don't ask. . .) along a prohibited and, as yet, unset tarmac road.

"*Interdit*" is French for forbidden, and in Algeria its use is as widespread as (insert preferred simile). You disregard it at your cost.

Over there a pile of earth had been pushed up across Algeria's principle highway and a sloppily painted sign read "Interdit – Route barée à 120k" – "Road closed for 80 miles". Not that the last eighty miles had been anything more than a succession of spoke-bending potholes and broken tarmac. From here to Tamanrasset the route would mainly follow sandy tracks, a chance to find out whether the Ténéré was worthy of its name.

As I beat the fossilised baguette with a ten-inch shifter, attempting to disengage a mouth-sized morsel, another bike pulled in and was quickly assessed. An old 900 BMW with a leaning tower of luggage on the back, anomalous junk strapped here and there and an angle of handlebar that combined to remind me of my first enthusiastic but unsuccessful venture into this region, four years ago.

However, I was looking for a partner for the three-day crossing to Niger, and this being the only other solo bike I'd seen, we agreed to meet in Tamanrasset in two days time. Whatever happened *this* time, I would not be alone. . .

Filling up with petrol and water, I headed out along the diversion through the Arak gorge. Try soft sand ruts, corrugations, and about an hour of 15mph rubble-road for starters and you'll be understandably relieved when the gorge fades out into a wide open sand plain where there is room to pick your way through the tricky bits.

I wound it wide open and hunted out the ruts and ridges in the featureless midday glare. All things considered, the XT coped really well. Riding here on an open class 'crosser would have been fun unlimited; it's really no harder, though less predictable that the Weston. But on 200kg of trail bike loaded up with "everything-I'll-need-for-the-next-two-months" and no ice cream van for at least 200 miles, you will appreciate that priorities lie with surviving the day; enjoyment is a welcome bonus.

Anyway, as long as the speed was kept up and all movements executed with premeditated delicacy, the big single was not too much of a handful. With cheeky optimism I previewed my arrival in Dakar in a few weeks time.

Sometime later the tracks ran parallel with, and even crossed the prohibited road. No barricades or signs, so I mounted the blacktop and settled down to a restfully vacant 70mph cruise and thought "That was a quick 120km, and why are those two 2CVs bogged in the sand down there when they could be up here".

Half an hour later I was getting my answer in the form of a faintly familiar bollocking. "How many kilometres have you driven on the closed road!?" demanded the agitated army officer.
"Er, about fifteen," I lied.
"Right, you spend fifteen days here! *Donnez-moi votre papiers*!"
Unwittingly, I blown it again. I tried to explain, "No barricades, no signs, speedo no work. . . " but it was all a waste of time and I prepared myself to endure a fortnights holiday in this geological zoo.
"Is there any water here?" I asked.
"NON!" he snapped.
"Oh, what a shame" I replied sarcastically, expecting to be dead by the New Year.

I joined the others who'd also got caught, mostly French students trying to do Tamanrasset on the cheap during their Christmas hols. "Fifteen days," I told them, and laughed. I hoped it would just be a couple, like last time. But, no sooner had I pulled out my water bottle for a needy sip, then the ear-bender let me go.

Confused, yet relieved by the outcome of his power games with us thoughtless tourists, I carried on winding my way through the sand and stones and next afternoon chugged contentedly down Tamanrasset High Street. Helmut, on the BMW, arrived later that evening, the thud-BOOM, thud-BOOM of his engine beat indicating the latest score:

Saharan corrugations – 1, Left-hand silencer mount – Nil.

After a few days, during which Christmas came and went like any other day in the desert, our bikes and bodies had received the rest and repairs they needed, and we were ready to leave Tam for the south.

Helmut, like myself, had since revised his original itinerary and now planned to cross the Sahara to Togo, sell his bike and fly home. A crash in the Hoggar mountains had further shaken the integrity of the ex-Politzei motoradd and now, as we rode off to fulfil our check-out duties with the authorities, it was clear that the rocky descent from Assekrem had done more damage than was apparent, as the fully overloaded sub-frame dragged against the back tyre over the slightest bump.

A block of two-by-four was found (at a price – "wood doesn't grow on trees out here!" explained the cheerful vendor) and we crammed in to lift the weight off the tyre. I also persuaded Helmut to get rid of his cherished guitar and tent, and took some gear on the back of my bike.

After a warning from the police that return to Tamanrasset "*est interdit*", we moved on to the Customs who eventually coughed up the necessary stamp and squiggle and let us loose with a handshake and a "*bonne route*".

The tarmac road that may eventually seal the Sahara from north to south sometime in the late 21st century, had grown about 25 miles since I last passed this way on my XT500 four years ago.

Soon after the asphalt turned to sand we camped around an upturned Peugeot wreck, hoping to cover the 200 miles to In Guezzam, the Algerian frontier post, in one long day. "*Ainsh Allah*", as they say out here when you talk of the future, meaning: "God willing. . .".

We were away by half eight next morning, soon striking up a good, fast pace on the mostly firm sandy tracks heading south. Over 60mph I was unable to match the high speed stability and sticky throttle of Helmut's BM and at this rate expected to be at the frontier by mid after-noon.

But then, around midday, we came across the consequence of

speeding over-confidently across the ever-changing desert terrain. Another BMW, this time a well prepared GS, rested on one pot while its unhurt rider applied tools to the other. The Swiss owner had left Tam a few hours before us, also accompanied by a Ténéré, and had looped a few loops in an unexpected patch of soft sand. The bike was remarkably undamaged but the cartwheeling had somehow flooded the cylinders, seizing the engine in some kind of hydraulic lock.

Fortunately Helmut has plenty of experience between the covers of Boxer engines and a couple of hours later, while the GS cleared its oily bores on a fast tickover, Swiss Michael thanked Helmut for his help and we split back into two pairs heading south.

Towards evening we ploughed our way into the deep sand around the "Dunes de Laouni" and watched our speedo needles sink into single figures. Our rear wheels churned out twenty foot roosts as we wove our way through the dunes looking for traction. In Guezzam would not see us tonight.

Another soft sand prang had further eroded Helmut's EEC Baggage Mountain. The poor bloke was knackered inside-out trying to keep the heavy road bike upright in this stuff. Yet spare a thought for the Kiwi we had seen in Tam a few days ago heading this way – two up on a one-litre RS! Expecting to find him and his pillion buried up to their indicators, we pressed on, hoping to relocate the main tracks we had mislaid before stopping for the night, so as to aid restful sleep.

"Just one more hill" I urged on the exhausted Helmut. One hill too many, alas. I caught up with his bike (having deviated briefly to investigate a friendly-looking tree) lying on its side, with Helmut cradling his right arm like a baby, broken at the shoulder.

"I Sink zis iz zi end" remarked the sentimental German as he looked down sorrowfully at his dying friend. The last of many rocks with "Helmut" written on them had taken out his front wheel in third and finally delivered the *coup de grace* to the ratty old twin. Petrol leaked from the tanks and oil from the engine. Even with lengthy bodges to get it running he'd still be unable to ride it. So, after a heartening meal and a spliff, I poured the gallons of spare fuel over the expired machine, stood back camera poised, and gave Helmut the matches. . .

Next morning realising that, yes, it had all really happened, I helped Helmut sort out what he could take and what he must leave. We chucked what bits of superfluous baggage he had onto the still-smouldering bike and attached the rest to ourselves and the XT.

By wobbling west for a few miles we relocated the main mass of corrugated southbound tracks we'd lost last night, and after a couple of hours of merciless thrashing to keep the overladen Ténéré skimming over the sand, we listened to it clicking itself cool outside the unexpected café at In Guezzam while we sipped on expensive Fantas.

Now rules are rules, and to a frontier official posted a 1000 miles from home where the summer mercury hits 55°C, abandoning an expired vehicle in the desert is strictly. . . *interdit*. The numerous wrecks we'd seen on the way here were clearly sculptures thoughtfully erected by the Ministry of Arts. They told Helmut, who was by now eating painkillers like Smarties, that he must recover his bike and bring it back – how, was his problem. This excessive demand was, after a few hours of cigarette swapping, negotiated down to a more reasonable "go down the nick and fill out a form".

That night was New Year's Eve and as we dozed uncomfortably in the sand, a drunken officer who had been doing a lot of anti-Imperialist ranting, came over and kicked the innocent Ténéré – his envy of my superb machine had obviously overwhelmed him. Helmut says "cool it" and gets threatened with the slammer. Meanwhile, in northern France the Paris–Dakar Rally was getting under way.

Next afternoon I left sunny Algeria to complete the final 150 mile leg of the desert crossing alone while Helmut waited for a supply plane to take him back to Tamanrasset and Europe before his shoulder set and his Smarties ran out.

Half an hour saw me over the thirty miles of No Man's Land (who'd want it?) to Assamaka, the Nigeran frontier post. Uncannily isolated and perched on a sandy hill surrounded by . . . sand, the place is little more than a tree, a dingy café and a Portacabin™ divided thrice between police, Customs and army. One of these swallowed my papers till the next morning, leaving me free to dream about cream cakes and toilet seats.

Luckily all was in order next morning (some without appropriate vaccination forms had to return to Tam) and at 8.30 I headed rather apprehensively into the southeastern void, following the intermittently spaced *bidons*.

In just 125 miles the tarmac resumed at the mining town of Arlit and I would be safely on the other side of the desert. But, of course, I should have known by now not to count my unhatched chickens because within an hour dickbrain had lost sight of the oil drums, the tracks and any faith in his observational skills. Later it occured to me that trying to read a magnetic compass while riding a steel-tanked bike was leading me astray. I stopped about halfway and got well away from the machine to take a bearing on anything to the east-southeast. Good job too as a couple of hundred yards back were my throwovers which had come adrift while bouncing through a particularly bumpy river bed. Another near disaster averted, I re-lashed the bags over the back of the seat and pointed my quivering fender towards that hint of a hill in the east.

At one point, as my bionic eye scanned the featureless horizon of a big arrow saying "THIS WAY", I was caught out by some talcum powder-like sand known as *feche-feche* which sucked down the front wheel and expelled me over the 'bars before I could even brake.

"One-two-five" clicked onto the now functioning odometre and there was still no sign of Arlit or the nearby Aïr mountains. The odd camel appeared and so did a few charred tree stumps which resembled the long-lost marked posts and lured me like flypaper. Out of nowhere a track appeared and was soon joined by another and soon the reassuring feel of corrugations under wheel signified "many vehicles come this way".

About one o'clock I spotted the uranium mine on Arlit's perimeter and thought at last, the end is nigh. And indeed it nearly was for a glance behind me to locate the source of the unusually high temperature warming my back revealed the rear of my bike shrouded in flames, cooking the loaded jerrican into an incendiary device worthy of a department store at Christmas.

As soon as I could fall off I wrenched the bulging can from the bike and slung it away and by the time the engine and petrol had been shut off, bits of burnt pannier and seat vinyl flaked off in the stiff breeze that fanned the fire. Fortunately there was plenty of that stuff you find on the beach with which to quell the flames and after some errant scooping I flopped down in the sand, unsure whether I'd just been very lucky or unlucky.

•

Two weeks later I rode the double-punctured bike across the shallow river that separated Mali from Senegal. Dakar (and a pair of inner tubes) was within my sights now, and as if I'd not already had enough, I was already planning my return to the desert.

(A version of the above feature originally appeared in the August 1986 edition of *SuperBike* magazine

SPOKE TOO SOON
By Peter Corbett

The End of the Road is an apt description for Illizi. Twelve hundred miles into the Algerian Sahara, at the farthest limit of the tarmac road, it is the first true desert town the traveller encounters on a trip south along the Libyan/Algerian border, and it was here that Chris and I had chosen to stop and change the Tyres of our Teneres in preparation for the rocky piste to come. Just a week into the trip, with the easy part completed of an ambitiously planned 7000 mile, six week epic into the remote reaches of the Sahara, it was to be the end of the road for me too. Examination of the bike's back wheel revealed that seven of the extra strong, heavy duty, go-anywhere spokes I had been so careful to use, had inexplicably broken and that despite the survival of the remaining twenty nine, any thoughts of carrying on were out of the question. I knew already that the efforts I would make to get it repaired would come to nothing, and that an uncertain journey back to Britain was the only immediate future I had.

Staring slack-jawed at the plate of spaghetti that had once been my back wheel, I began to ponder my return home. It had all seemed so seductive only weeks before as I finalised my few sponsorships. Personal ads in the press seeking partners had unearthed a motley brigade of potential compadres, whittled down eventually to the one correspondent with significant experience, and scores of letters had gleaned support from only Castrol, Frank Thomas, Mitsui and Lorus Quartz. Preparation had been carried out over months to the nth degreed now it all seemed so worthless.

Chris had himself faced a similar situation six years earlier on a solo trip south of the Hoggar Mountains in the central Sahara. His specially made alloy tank had split, leaving him lost and vulnerable, and the experience gave him a kind of stoicism about the crisis. Despite the fact that all his plans for taking on the remote and dangerous Tenere desert would now have to be abandoned, he cheerily insisted on laying me out corpse-style and taking my picture with the offending wheel as a headstone. The eventual decision was that he would carry on alone on a much abbreviated journey, and with Christmas looming, I would need to be back in Algiers within three days if I was not to be stranded by the holiday closedown. We spent the rest of the day changing the tyres anyway and made a small fire from Acacia branches before turning in for a fitful night's sleep

Morning revealed that the scratching I had heard next to my ear during the night had not been the Spoke Fairy mending the wheel after all, but a gerbil hollowing out the loaf I had left out as an offering to the gods. The wheel looked no better no matter how hard I looked at it, and the ferry at Algiers was certainly no nearer than it had been the night before. Twelve hundred miles of desert, an extremely iffy back wheel and three days to complete the lot if I wasn't to be stranded by the Christmas shutdown was the menu for the foreseeable future. The old tyres were chucked up the Acacia tree for the benefit of any passing traveller who might need them, Chris and I said our farewells, and as the Sun rose uncomfortably high in the sky, I pointed the Tenere back north and sighed deeply.

Half a mile out of Illizi, as my speed rose to about 50mph, the bike suddenly launched itself into a massive reservoir frappeur (as we had come to call such handling peccadilloes in French-speaking Algeria). As the back wheel spat from side to side and the fearsome slo-mo view of things came into play, I found myself with time to ponder the consequences of a major accident so far from home and the prospect of Algerian hospital food. What I ended up with was a gradual detente of the jiggery pokery and a cold sweat at the side of the road.

The problem turned out to be a buckled front wheel, earned no doubt during a recent spill in soft sand. A spoke key was enough to put it right. Just to emphasise the point, the Sun rose a little more in the sky and, with a hundred and fifty miles just to the nearest town, the task of clocking up twelve hundred-odd of the little bastards in almost no time at all seemed a remote prospect to say the least. Nevertheless, with the front wheel now behaving itself and the dunes of the Erg Isseiouane behind me, the familiar shape of In Amenas, a largish oil town, hoved into view and I pulled in for some water and a think. As I sat frying in the square, an ancient British ex-army truck and trailer parked and disgorged its load of eurotrekkies into the nearby shop. A quick conversation with the driver revealed that they were heading South rather than the hoped-for North, so with a disconsolate shrug I turned back to the bike and steeled myself for the miles to come. Taking pity on my plight, and being, as it turned out, an ex-biker with many problem-filled miles behind him on a Honda 400/4 in Kathmandu, the driver called me back and offered a night's pick of the wealth of facilities hidden within the truck. These comprised beer, shepherd's pie, chocolate pudding, a tent and a bed, and it took me no time at all to decide on the offer's points victory over my own miserable alternative of dossing on the ground, eating dehydrated food and scraping the usual ice of my sleeping bag in the morning. I stayed the night and decided to sod the consequences of the lost hundred or so miles I would otherwise have clocked up had I stayed on the road.

A few miles out in the desert and feeling suitably sated on absolute lashings of chocolate pudding, Lapsed into a comfortable torpor and sat listening to the banter of the trekkies in the cool of the desert night. A large jackal, numbed no doubt by the stupefying hunger that pervades most species of fauna in the Sahara, approached the camp, feigning attacks and retreating confused behind the torch beams shone at it from the polyglot ranks of the trekkies. A gendarme appeared from nowhere, demanding passports and whisky and regaled the timorous bunch with stories of a fatal attack by a similar beast on a woman the previous year.

I turned in and zipped my tent up tight.

The next day brought the realisation that there was still the small matter of about a thousand miles between me and the relative safety of Algiers and that, despite feeling a whole lot better for the food and rest, I had a definite need to get stuck in if I was to make the Marseilles ferry the following afternoon. What was worse was that most of it would need to be completed in the first day if I was to leave myself with enough leeway for an afternoon sailing the day after. A quick glimpse at the map showed that Ghardaia, another large oasis town, was about 650 miles away, and with only ten hours of daylight to do it in, the prospects of a leisurely canter across the desert were diminishing by the minute. On a big road bike I would have had worries: on a Tenere with a back wheel about to cast off its mortal coil, I was nigh on catatonic.

My first fill up at Hassi Bel Guebbour (me chocolate, the bike petrol) told me that the bike was using far more fuel than on the way out. I put the problem down to a stiff headwind and the fatter Michelins, although as I was to find out later, it may have been more to do with the latter's contact with the bike's after market side stand, and this taught me Lesson Number One - try out all modifications to the bike before you leave home. I kept a special watch out for the potholes that had probably started the rot in the first place and soon learned to pick out the black streaks laid down by four wheelers whose drivers saw the chasms too late. Some, seriously deep, stretched the whole width of the road and with no way round, I had to come to a virtual halt and treat them motocross-style, whooping gloriously out of the far edge, foot off the rest and waving to the crowd (of lizards). Such diversions were sparse. Various animals scattered from the side of the road, including camels and a pair of rare mouflons, a kind of heavy-horned desert sheep, more familiarly seen in mountain garb, sledge hammering away at like-minded numskulls on the alpine slopes.

Mile after dry mile rattled past and before long the distance began to make itself felt. Not through the saddle, which was surprisingly comfortable, but because of the spinnaker-like riding position. Later in the day, as the Sun settled down towards the horizon and my rest stops became more frequent, a noticeable and worrying noise developed around the back wheel area. More out of hope than anything else, I adjusted the chain and pretended the noise had gone away. It hadn't, but by this time the distance to Ghardaia had dropped to a reachable level and I decided to carry on into the night rather than drag myself off through the dark to a hassle-free distance from the road. Ghardaia was still 300 km away though, and after darkness fell and the only sights were the lights of the occasional passing truck, I began to hallucinate and formed in my mind's eye a tunnel of trees wrapped around the barren darkness at the side of the road. The back wheel continued to rattle audibly, even at speed, but in my state of near delirium, I pressed on, barely caring. The descending figures on the mileage signs gave me the only incentive to keep going and after the last hundred kilometres had dragged themselves painfully slowly through the final stages of the day, Ghardaia lit up before me and, in a state of complete mental detachment, I rattled up a dusty dual carriageway and into town.

Dragging myself into the first hotel I came to, I was given a half built room for a tenner. It was terrible, but I'd have paid double for much worse. I asked for somewhere to put the bike and was shown through a pair of double doors. Through the dust, a dim light bulb hanging from a bent flex lit up the haze and revealed a large garage containing two cars. Round the walls, young men surrounded by their possessions lay on mattresses and looked up at me listlessly as I parked the bike in their living accommodation.

The manager had told me I could only have the room for one night, so after a poor sleep, I got up, peeled open the single scab I had once known as a pair of lips and went downstairs to inspect the bike. It took no time to realise that it would never make it to Algiers. Several more spokes were broken, the remaining few were largely loose, and selective tightening came nowhere near spreading the load enough to make it safe. A swift round of all the local mechanics and moped shops told me what I already knew, i.e. that a repair was impossible. I would have to find another way of getting back and guessing that, as with all things Algerian, there was no way it would take one day when two would do nicely, I set about looking for another room. Everywhere was full except for one dingy lodging house where I was offered a bathroom. Tiles on the walls, no window, a board on the bath with a mattress on top, no water in the taps and a gang of chummy looking cockroaches on the floor. It was close to Christmas, there was barely any room at this inn, and the festive analogy wasn't hard to conjure up. I inspected the toilet down the hall and decided that if I wanted to use it, I'd have to stand in the corridor to do so, the whole floor was so piled with filth. All this plus the usual routine from the manager that Europeans get everywhere in Algeria.

"Sell me your bike; it's much better than mine" (an ancient non-functioning BMW R60)

"All right then, buy this camera" (a free-with-four-gallons plastic number that didn't work).

"No? Then sell me the mirrors off your bike. Yes, I know I already have some, but yours are so much better. No, no, don't go away. Sell me your helmet. All right, I'm sorry. Please come back."

I wandered round the back streets for a while and picked my way through the dead cats, dead rats and rats' heads left by cats. Eventually I fell across a square of the ubiquitous Peugeot 404 pickups used throughout the Sahara. I guessed that some of the drivers must make regular trips to replenish the market stalls in the Souk and had banked on offering about £40-£50 for a ride on the 375 mile trip. The story was the same wherever I went. "To you, a special price- 3600 dinars". About £400. My European looks obviously meant more to them than me about my apparent wealth and I wondered around some more, touting myself around the lorry drivers without any success and coming up with no better ideas at the small tourist office. By this time I was willing to try anything and for no good reason shuffled into the Air Algeria office, drawn by the seductive travel posters of alpine scenes.

"How much for a ticket to Algiers, single?"

"Two hundred and twenty-six Dinars." (about twenty-six pounds)

I stared at the clerk for a second or two, and as the words "Open Sesame" sprung to mind, I hardly dared ask the follow-up question..

"I have about two hundred kilos of excess luggage. C'est une probleme?"

After a quarter of an hour of chat and a few minutes with a calculator, a total price of 409 Dinars for me and the bike was arrived at - about £47. I'd need to change sufficient funds at the bank in the morning, and the plane would leave at noon the next day, covering the equivalent of London to Glasgow for a relative pittance.

I left the office wearing a silly grin and set of to look for somewhere to eat a celebratory meal. A friendly looking restaurant was open and I asked what they had. On offer was cous cous, lambs' hearts or fish, all with rice, cauliflower, chips or green beans. I ordered fish, chips and green beans and sat waiting for my food. Only seconds later, the dish arrived. It looked appetising. I cut up the sardine-like fish, speared a chip and some haricots and put the lot in my mouth. It was stone cold. A row of similarly-piled plates looked down at me from the shelf above, waiting for future customers.

The whole town closed down at about eight. I returned to my bath-bed, and after a fitful night on the tiles, I was up early to catch the bank and change the money I needed. As I waited for it to open, a gang of boys aged about fourteen worked outside on the pavement laying flagstones. Across the road, a Renault 4 started up and for some reason lurched straight into the back of a lorry, bursting the windscreen and buckling the door pillars. The boys collapsed together in laughter, slapping the ground with their hands, barely able to catch their breath. One of them, tears rolling down his cheeks, wrenched open the nearside door and released the bewildered driver. The bank opened ten minutes early and within minutes I had the currency and the necessary tickets.

The ten miles to the airport proved too much for the damaged wheel and I arrived with its new found eccentricity inviting strange looks as it lurched sideways with every turn. Quite why the wheel chose now, only ten miles after a 650 mile dash across a hostile, barren desert to complete its demise is a matter entirely between me and the Grim Reaper. I barely dared contemplate it and concentrated instead on working the bike through the treacle-like bureaucracy. The tank was emptied, the tyres were deflated to prevent explosion in the uncompressed hold and an unlucky baggage handler was given the job of pushing it in this state to the Boeing 727 waiting on the tarmac. A practised team lifted it bodily up the six feet or so into the aircraft and I boarded the plane in a state of bemused euphoria.

Rain greeted me in Algiers and I waited an hour and a half for freight workers to retrieve the bike from the plane. It eventually arrived lying on its side on the blades of a fork lift truck and was lowered gently to the ground in front of me. The gear lever was folded neatly under the engine casing and the clutch lever pointed skywards. A bag of rice was missing from one of the pouches. I pumped up the tyres and took a jerry can off to find some petrol. Half an hour later I was wobbling through the Dantean hubbub of Algiers where, miraculously, a ferry to Marseilles was leaving in an hour. Still unable to believe there was any steak and kidney left in my good luck pie, I boarded the ship where I met a Paris-Dakar biker on his way back from a final shakedown test in the desert before the off the following week. He shook his head at the sorry state of my spokes and pointed to his own to indicate that I should have wired them together at their juncture. In a haze of incredulous relief, I didn't care what he had to say and instead got stuck into filling out the numerous duplicate forms needed for almost any official movement in Algeria.

The twenty-four hour trip to Marseilles was an uncomfortable one of spit, sleaze and leer. As the only European travelling steerage, I was the subject of constant disdain by increasingly drunk Algerians who dipped further into the Pernod the further they got from their dry homeland. France arrived somewhere around the end of my soft European tether and the overflowing of the toilets. As I lurched out of the docks, Paris/Dakar man (who had been travelling first class, naturally) launched past me, front wheel pawing the air. Impressed (honest..), I continued in my snail-like pace the mile or so towards the station and the Paris train. As I arrived, the Desert Bolide wheelied past me again and dismounted, rubbing his knee. It seemed one wheelie too many had caught him out in the Marseilles traffic and given him a heavy hint for the weeks to come. Wonder if he made it through that first desert section.

The rest of the trip involved a series of trains, a ferry and a hire van in which I was accompanied to Calais by a Europcar clerk, the epony-mously named Eric Welcome, who came with me so he could visit his mother in Lille on Christmas Day and save me sixty quid by returning the van to Paris. The only time I was totally stranded in the whole trip was at Dover on Boxing Day when there wasn't a train or bus to be had, and in essence, that summed up the whole trip. Equally unexpected good bad luck in unpredictable doses at about the level of a made-for-

TV movie. On the basis that I'd exhausted a sizeable chunk of my lifetime's bad luck, it seemed churlish not to go again. Doing in the dunes what bears do in the woods is a quickly acquired skill even for softies like me, and a Tenere, especially the electric start version, really wasn't the he-man bike I had imagined

As for Chris, he arrived home two weeks later than me after an uneventful trip through the spectacular Hoggar Mountains and a return up the main trans-Sahara highway. His spokes, identical to mine, had caused him no problems on far worse roads than anything I had had to put up with and he had completed his first crisis-free Saharan trip. I had to wait till the next year for another go at mine.

BOOKS

This is a selection of some of the books about the Sahara and motorbiking that I've read over the years. No price indicates that a book is no longer in print but is listed as it may be available from a public library or secondhand bookshop.

AFRICA ON A SHOESTRING Geoff Crowther et al (Lonely Planet). £16.99. Now in its eighth edition, this book accomplishes the monumental task of detailing all of Africa's 41 countries and is better than might be expected. A useful space saver for a trans African trip. There are around eleven other LPs covering African regions and countries.

ALGERIA AND THE SAHARA by Val and Jon Stevens (Constable). Those were the days, in the late Sixties, when the rather eccentric Stevens pair could bomb around the Sahara alone in their SWB Land Rover, with a courteous salute from the obliging authorities. *Algeria and the Sahara* is a bright and enthusiastic guide to a bygone Golden Age of Saharan motoring. Jon Stevens was also a bit of a scooter buff, writing three titles culminating in the seminal *The Scooter; A Complete Guide*.

ALGERISCHE SAHARA by U.&W. Eckbert (Dumont). Although the only word I recognise is 'Sahara', this looks as good a guide to the Algerian Sahara as there is, by Europe's most motivated and intrepid travelling nation. With typical attention to detail and excellent background, it includes full accounts of some remote pistes as well as details on 4x4 preparation. But, like the Sahara Handbook, there's very little on motorbikes.

ARABIAN SANDS by Wilfred Thesiger (Penguin). £6.99. An account of Thesiger's camelback crossings of Saudi's Empty Quarter in the late 1940s, just before the discovery of oil changed the way of life there forever. The book details the life and hardships among the nomads and lands that he loved. It clearly explores the Bedouin's fierce desire for freedom which extends far beyond matters of personal comfort, or even life itself. A desert classic. Thesiger's autobiography, *A Life of My Choice* says it all.

The slim, attractive hard-back '**AUJOURD'HUI**' series of glossy travel guides, published by Les Editions J A., include all the countries of former French West Africa. Colourful and descriptive, rather than practical, they give a 'National Geographic' type overview of the country in question. These books have a fairly flowery writing style hinting at the coffee table rather than the tank bag. Available for around £18 from Stanfords or the Travel Bookshop (see Useful Addresses).

CONQUEST OF THE SAHARA by Douglas Porch (Oxford University Press). An intriguing and readable account of France's attempts to colonise the Sahara during the 'Race for Africa' in the latter half of the 19th century. Full of historical detail, it vividly describes the vainglorious expeditions, large and small, which struggled across the Sahara, often poorly led and suffering greatly for personal prestige and their country's honour. The extraordinary shambles of the doomed Flatters' expeditions has to be read to be believed.

DAY TRIPS TO THE DESERT by Geoff Nicholson (Sceptre) £5.99. Accomplished fiction writer Geoff wangles an advance from his publisher to try something different; travel around and write a book about visiting deserts – an environment that has always fascinated him. The wry, personal account of trips to the Moroccan Sahara, Egypt, the Outback and the southwest US is leadened by the trauma of his father's slow death back in England. Although he amusingly describes the strange encounters that seem to befall visitors to desert places, as the title suggests, he doesn't really explore them or their enigma with the intellectual vigour they deserve. Altogether an overly lighthearted approach to an important subject!

DESERT ENCOUNTER by Knut Holmboe (Quilliam). £8.95. Knut was a Dane who converted to Islam and set out to drive on a hadj (pilgrimage) to Mecca. The book describes the most dangerous part of his journey across North Africa from Morocco to Cairo in 1935. All sorts of misfortunes befell him on his way to Mecca including arrest, bandit attack and nearly dying of thirst, when he left the immobilised car to search for help, but his determination and faith saw him through. Sadly he was ambushed and killed in the Middle East during his second hadj.

FEARFUL VOID by Geoffrey Moorhouse (Sceptre). £5.99. In the early Seventies Moorhouse set off to be the first to walk across the Sahara from west to east and while do so, to "test his fear of death", something just as easily achieved by playing croquet on the M25. His book is a good example of monumentally crass westerners' using the Sahara or Africa as a backdrop for their own improbable and egotistical stunts. (*Wheelbarrow Across The Sahara* by Geoffrey Someone is a still more asinine tale.) Plenty of people were dying in the Sahara at that time, proving nothing more than the need for water during severe drought. Moorhouse utterly underestimated his undertaking and knew little the environment or of the people he needed to achieve his goal. Irritated that his guides' dallying with passing nomads would mess up his schedule, he got what he deserved: ripped-off and running with dysentry, he scrapped through to Tamanrasset and went home with a big sword. A great story and still in print.

FLYAWAY by Desmond Bagley (Harper Collins). £4.99. Geographically authentic, fast-paced thriller set in the Hoggar, Ténéré and Tassili of the central Sahara. Tintin for grown-ups, where laconic heroes like Byrne say "What the Hell..." a lot, and casually swop diffs' in sandstorms, while chased by mysterious assassins. Women are usually someone else's sister and 'strangely attractive'. Infuriatingly compulsive departure lounge stuff. By comparison Clive Cussler's similarly adventuresome **SAHARA** (Grafton; £5.99) is a load of preposterous and implausible rubbish with a feeble eco-message – easily unfinishable and a waste of a good title!

GUIDE DU SAHARA by B. Vaes, Gerard del Marmol and Albert d'Otreppe (Hachette). A guide to the French Sahara, this is in some ways better, in others inferior, to the ageing Sahara Handbook. The latest, imported edition costs nearly £25 from UK bookshops. Less comprehensive on vehicle preparation, while avoiding some of the Handbook's padding, it's a useful supplement for those fluent in French. Includes in depth, country-by-country details (including Chad), but is spoilt by maps drawn by a five-year-old.

IMPOSSIBLE JOURNEY by Michael Asher (Penguin). £6.99. Asher is a modern-day Thesiger, with a similar distrust of cars and love for the desert and its people. In 1986, accompanied by his newly-wed wife, Marianetta (who photographed their journey), he succeeded in completing Geoffrey Moorhouse's (see *Fearful Void*) failed attempt to cross the Sahara from Mauritania to the Nile. Setting a gruelling pace that even some of the guides found tough, the Ashers, unlike

Moorhouse, had lived in the desert for some years and the author was familiar with nomadic customs, selection of guides and the all-important purchase and care of camels. These factors, added to the couples' enormous physical and mental stamina, helped in their successful attempt to be the first Westerners to complete this feat of endurance. The mentally disorientating ego loss and intolerable stress they experienced towards the end of the trip comes close to some of the *Sheltering Sky*'s themes.   It's as well to remember that countless Moors and other pilgrims may have completed this trek on their way to Mecca over the past thousand years. As one perplexed Nigeran border official ruefully observed, "What will you Westerners think of next?".

IN SEARCH OF THE SAHARA, by Quentin Crewe (Michael Joseph). A mixed group of privileged wanderers journey all over the Sahara in a pair of Unimogs, led by the author's scholarly interest. It's rather spoilt by his sneering attitude towards other travellers; in Crewe's words "appropriately named 'overlanders' because they skim the surface". Snobbery among travellers is a common failing; perhaps the 'overlanders' may not have been inclined or able to mount a year-long private expedition in the Sahara with a bunch of extravagant vehicles. The book nearly explores the juicy topic of group dynamics, much more interesting to the casual reader than ancient tombs.

IN SEARCH OF THE TASSILI FRESCOES by Henri Lhote (Hutchinson). Essential and illuminating reading for anyone considering visiting the 'open air museum' of prehistoric rock art on the plateau above Djanet in southeastern Algeria. It explains how the late Lhote (the acknowledged expert on ancient Saharan art) and a group of talented amateur artists spent over a year on the plateau. With the aid of air drops (the Tassili is beyond the reach of cars), they studiously copied the unique artistic treasure for posterity. Their work may still be on display at the Museum of Mankind in Paris.

JUPITER'S TRAVELS by Ted Simon (Penguin). £5.99. *The* Round-the-World biking classic that has probably launched more Big Trips in bikers' beer-charged imaginations than any other book. Ted Simon writes with a mellow, humane and adventurous approach: "if things get dull, just run out of petrol" he suggests - don't try this in the Sahara. The out-of-date, low-tech wisdom of his ways is still summarised in Wexas' otherwise comprehensive *Traveller's Handbook*. He may not have known much about bikes, and his Triumph was rebuilt several times, but so far, no one has said it better and with such universal appeal. A sequel, *Riding Home*, surfs rather limply on the original's enduring popularity.

LIBYAN SANDS by R.A. Bagnold (Michael Haag). £5.95. Ralph Bagnold recalls some of the earliest motor-car adventures and explorations in the eastern Sahara while stationed in Egypt in the 1920s. Using Model T Fords, Ralph and his chums spent every spare moment of leave exploring the Libyan Desert of Egypt and northern Sudan. His passionate enthusiasm for (often literally) pushing the spindly, steaming Fords across uncharted *ergs*, helped develop the techniques which are standard practice today in desert driving.   Ralph Bagnold went on to write *The Physics of Blown Sand*, the definitive account of sand formations and features, (for geological graduates only). At the beginning of the World War II, he also helped set up the audacious Long Range Desert Group, an independently mobile 'private army' of saboteurs who rained havoc behind enemy lines in Libya, later carrying the newly formed Special Air Service on some of their earliest raids.

MOTORRAD ABENTEUER TOUREN by Bernd Tesch (Globetrott-Zentrale) Bernd Tesch is mad about bike travel and bikers' travels. He's spent years tracking down every book written about bike touring and interviewed their authors where possible. This book is the result of that work, an anthology of 262 books published since 1910. If you share his enthusiasm and can read German, you'll love it. If you can only read German then you might find Tesch's **AFRIKA MOTORRAD REISEN** useful. It covers more or less the same information as *Desert Biking* but on an African scale. The layout is a bit unsophisticated, but 25,000 have been sold since it came out in 1976. Both of these books (as well as selected desert biking gear) are available for around DM30 from Tesch's HQ; see Useful Addresses.

MOTORRAD REISEN by Thomas Trossman (Reisebuch-Verlags-GmbH). Although mostly oriented around the author's vast experience of biking in the Sahara, this sandbuch (as the cover dryly suggests) offers advice on adventurous biking all over the world. With some great photographs and twenty pages devoted to outrageous-engined sidecars, just looking at this excellently-produced guide makes you want to get on your bike and go. Trossmann has also written a couple of books about his own bike travels in the desert: *Wustenzeit Sahara grenzenlos*, a report on nearly three years of accumulated biking in the Sahara; *Der Wüste begegnen*, about all his travels in the desert with some great photos, and *Wüstenfahrer* subtitled 'With a Motorbike in the Land of the Tuaregs'. These titles are available from the author who also organises bike tours in the Sahara (see Useful Addresses).

THE PASSIONATE NOMAD by Isabelle Eberhart (Virago). £6.99. The diary of a restless and depressive woman who wandered around North Africa at the beginning of this century, disguised as a man. After converting to Islam and marrying an Algerian, Eberhart lived occasionally in Ouargla, pursuing a life of self-destructive hedonism, spurred by a defiant love of the desert. "*I was already a nomad as a young girl*", she wrote, "*for me it seems that by advancing into unknown territories, I enter into my life*". She was drowned in a flash flood, aged only 27, and her posthumously published diaries soon became a feminist classic.

RUNNING WITH THE MOON – A Boy's Own Adventure by Jonny Bealby (Heinemann). £15.99. Claiming somewhat improbably to be the first such achievement, Jonny Bealby rides his Ténéré around Africa the hard way to help come to terms with his fiancée's tragic death. With his partner crashing out early the author continues alone, crossing the Sahara just ahead of the border closure in late-1991 but soon ditching the "easy" overlanders' route for a less predictable detour through Congo and Angola to the Cape. Pausing here for a beer and a new piston ring, he returns up Africa's east side to Cairo and the hope of fulfilling a romance initiated in Tamanrasset. Bealby's arduous trek is packed with the reciprocating gusts of fortune and misery that make African travel so draining and so memorable – although at times he did seek out danger for its own sake. Several times during the journey a place he'd just visited descended into bloodshed and warfare, but with guile and determination, a fair share of uncanny luck (plus the XT's legendary reliability) he completed his trip and was ultimately married. *Running With The Moon* may not be the new *Jupiter's Travels* – like many travelogues it suffers from the "if-it's-Tuesday-it-must-be- Malawi" syndrome. It's at its best when Bealby's up against it; slogging up to his waist and hitching canoe rides through the rainforest, or racing across Ethiopia's bandit country to confront Sudan's excruciating bureaucracy at 54°C. Here the pace cranks up as clichés are hurriedly discarded and a bit of laconic humour finally creeps. If you've ever thought of doing something similar this book will probably confirm your worst fears. A story of courage, road surface reports and True Love.

SAHARA by Jeremy Swift (Time Life International). £17.99. This is a splendidly illustrated and informative account of the geography of the Sahara, part of the otherwise seemingly lightweight series from Time Life covering 'The World's Wild Places'. Includes accounts of the Great Explorers' quests, descriptions of wildlife and geology as well as travels with nomads. Originally published in 1975, it's still in print and worth buying.

SAHARA by John Julius Norwich (Collins). A Golden Age of Sahara Motoring travelogue which describes a six week journey from Djanet to the Tibesti Mountains in Chad in 1968, a route that has long since been closed. Norwich, an author of many classical studies, does not claim to be a total fan of the Sahara - along with an other famed classicist, Peter Corbett, he found the nights too cold. However, by joining the expedition at the eleventh hour, when all the organising was done, he was able to devote his mind to making pertinent observations about the nature of the desert experience. Worth reading.

SAHARA HANDBOOK by Simon Glen (Lascelles) £18.95. Despite being in its third edition (1990) some parts of this book, especially the chapter on 'Two Wheels', are nearly as old as the Sahara itself. Nevertheless, it is still the Bible for Saharan enthusiasts and the most comprehensive book of its kind in English. It includes a very thorough section on the preparation of the commonly used cars in the Sahara, but it's not made clear later that some of the routes described have long been closed or are forbidden without a guide. Indispensible for any serious Saharan journey.

SAHARA, THE GREAT DESERT by E.F. Gautier (Hippocrene, New York) £8.99. Written in 1935, this was one of the first, modern accounts of the history and geography of the Sahara, by one of its most knowledgeable and eminent scholars. The original French version has been translated into English and is available cheaply in paperback.

SAI BILMA by Mike Foster (available from Travellers' Bookshop). £8.95. Privately published, low-key account of one of the last salt caravans to cross the Ténéré Desert in the early Seventies, before the Niger government was compelled to erect *balises* along the route. The author is an expert on the Ténéré region, and modestly underplays the drama that nearly finished off the caravan. Compare this with the self-agrandizing but more sensational (and marketable) *Fearful Void* or *Impossible Journey.*

SHELTERING SKY by Paul Bowles (Paladin). £5.99. A cult novel by the Tangiers literary guru based on the author's own experiences in North Africa. Not a thoughtful gift for a nervy visitor to Morocco, but a thrilling read if you like your desert with a bit of sex, madness, infidelity and death. Bertolucci's eponymous film is a hackneyed, desert romance, with dashing Tuareg princes, graceful caravans crossing golden dunes, and ululating tribeswomen at every turn. While certainly good-looking (filmed partly in the Ténéré), it fails to get its teeth into the inscrutable, existential quandaries of the protagonists. The track from the Police's *Synchronicity* album, *Tea in the Sahara*, relates a morbid legend described in this book.

SMITH & SON by Anthony Smith (Ulverscoft Large Print Books). £7.95. Thirty years on, Dad pulls his trusty old Triumph out of the shed to retrace his route back to the Cape. Only this time he takes his nineteen-year old 'first born' with him on another Tiger Cub. "Gee, thanks Dad?" Great idea for a book with a novel variation on the 'In the footsteps of. . . (myself)' theme, it's an amusing, charming and erudite travellers' tale, full of the terrors, wonders and memorable encounters that make Africa such a unique experience.

THROUGH AFRICA, AN OVERLANDERS GUIDE by Bob Swain and Paula Snyder (Bradt) £12.95. This excellent guide to driving, riding, cycling and overland-trucking across Africa includes a good section on bike preparation followed by a fairly lightweight, country-by-country guide and all interspersed with illuminating travel narratives.

TRAVELS IN MAURITANIA by Peter Hudson (Virgin). £14.99. A rather bland account of the author's travels in this fascinating and obscure country, the 'Albania of Africa'. Avoiding the wearying 'journey into myself' trend rather too painstakingly, Hudson remains scrupulously objective and, as a result, fails to satisfactorily express the curiosity and wonder that presumably drove him there in the first place. Peter Hudson also wrote *Two Rivers*, a moped journey from Dakar to Timbuktu and beyond – remaindered copies may still be available at the Travellers' Bookshop.

TREK by Paul Stewart (Cape). £14.99. An eerie coincidence whilst on holiday in Kenya leads the author to investigate the background and events of a trip undertaken by a mixed party of Brits in 1955. The sobering, 'factionalised' account details the foursome's tragic journey from Kenya back to Britain in a Morris Traveller. The fate of the woefully unprepared group (even the pet mongoose mascot was crushed in an accident) is illustrated with grainy shots of the horrifying climax near Assamaka, on the Niger frontier. It's a fascinating and frightening read, because these sort of tragedies can, and still do occur today. Would make a great subject for the sort of film they don't make any more.

TUAREG by Jeremy Keenan (Allen Lane). A seminal anthropological study of the customs, culture and lives of the Ahaggar Tuareg of southern Algeria's Hoggar Mountains. A specialist read, rather than an informative dip, if you want to know about Tuareg society and traditions inside out, this is the book, although Lord Rennell of Rod's *People of the Veil*, studying the Aïr Tuareg and published in the 1920s, is also worth searching for.

WEST AFRICA: THE ROUGH GUIDE by Jim Hudgens and Richard Trillo (Rough Guides). £15.99. Huge brick of a book due in autumn 1995, covering 18 countries from Cameroon to Mauritania in immense practical and historical detail. Boxes feature useful phrases in local languages and dialects. There are also Rough Guides to Morocco, Tunisia, Egypt, Kenya and Zimbabwe & Botswana.

WIND, SAND AND STARS by Antoine de Saint Exupery (Penguin). £4.99. An existential adventure classic based on the author's semi-autobiographical escapades in the early days of commercial aviation, which included flying mail across the dreaded Terres des Hommes (the Western Sahara) where you saved the last bullet for yourself, to the French administrative capital at Dakar. It features the almost obligatory near-death from-thirst experience after crashing in the Libyan Desert. Heroic and philosophically poetic Man's Stuff; Hemingway with propellers.

ZEN AND THE ART OF MOTORCYCLE MAINTENANCE

by Robert Pirsig (Vantage). £6.99. This was once the book to be seen reading on the tube, a baffling cult classic that many bikers understandably attempt. Still popular, I think the gist was "If it works, don't meddle". I have hereby saved you a long and impenetrable slog. Other holistic titles in the 'Zen and the Art of. . .' series failed to materialise.

INDEX

B

C

F

G

H

I